Adoption
Healing

Also by Joe Soll:

Adoption Healing...a path to recovery for mothers who lost babies to adoption, with Karen Buterbaugh Wilson (2003)

Evil Exchange, with Lori Paris (future)

Adoption Healing

...a path to recovery

Second Edition

Joe Soll, LCSW

GATEWAY PRESS, INC.
Baltimore, MD   2005

Cover design by Darlene Gerow

Please direct all correspondence and book orders to:
Joe Soll, LCSW
74 Lakewood Drive
Congers, NY 10920

First printing, Baltimore, 2000
Second printing, Baltimore, 2005

Library of Congress Cataloging-in-Publication Data
Soll, Joe, 1939-
    Adoption healing: a path to recovery / Joe Soll.
      p.cm.
    Includes bibliographical references.
    ISBN 0-9678390-0-9
    1. Adoption--Psychological aspects. 2. Adoptees--Psychology. 3.
Adopted children--Psychology. 4. Psychic trauma. 5. Psychotherapy. I.
Title.

HV875.S644 2000
362.73'4--dc21   00-023256

Published for the author by
Gateway Press, Inc.
3600 Clipper Mill Rd., Suite 260
Baltimore, MD 21211-1953

Printed in the United States of America

Dedication

To my natural mother,
whoever and wherever she is,
with love,
and to all those who either
are or were
Missing in Adoption.

Contents

Author's Notes:

I've worked with almost as many natural mothers[1] as adoptees and it is clear to me that the psychological experiences of the adoptee and the natural mother when they are separated are almost identical. The aftermath, the effects of their experience on their lives, runs a parallel course for both adoptees and natural mothers.

> Adoptees and their natural mothers experience "a shared trauma, a shared devastation and a shared potential for healing... Many natural mothers will be reading this book, and the whole way through may be saying, 'I FEEL like this, TOO. That's ME!' I felt 'empty' in moments as I read this book. I 'felt' the adoptee's VOID." – Jane Guttman

The natural mother experience has, for the most part, been unheard, unacknowledged by society, yet the effects of the loss of their babies is life-long and profound, and needs to be understood.

My intent when I started to write this book was to create a work to help both adoptees and natural mothers. While I decided to

---

[1] The term "natural mother" is used to describe a woman who has surrendered her child to adoption, not a woman who is pregnant.

focus on healing for the adoptee, the steps necessary for natural mothers to heal are almost identical. I hope that the natural mothers who read this book will be able to interpolate and use some of the healing methods presented herein for themselves.

As you read this book, no matter what your life experience has been, you may well become emotionally stimulated and experience feelings of anxiety, pain and sadness. Please know that this is normal and that you are not alone in your feelings. In the United States, referring only to non-kinship adoption, there are six million adoptees, twelve million natural parents and twelve million adoptive parents; thirty million people intimately involved in every adoption.

Finally, for convenience, I have chosen to use feminine pronouns throughout the book. There are an equal number of men involved in adoption and it is not my intent to exclude them by my use of the feminine pronouns. Also for convenience, I use the term adoptive parents to include prospective adoptive parents as well as those parents who have already adopted a child.

Acknowledgments

I would like to thank the many individuals without whom this book would not have been written. My sister Susan who finally told me the truth about a lie, the truth that set me free. My brother Ray, his wife Maureen and the rest of my adoptive family for supporting me along the way. Mary Sussillo whose infinite patience finally allowed me to lower my walls and deal with my feelings. Diana who has remained a constant light in my life for almost four decades.

Professor Robert Chazin, my personal guide; Annette Baran, Reuben Pannor and Joyce Maguire Pavao for their encouragement along the way; Nancy Verrier for her wisdom and courage in writing *The Primal Wound*; Betty Jean Lifton, for her wonderful books and endless knowledge; Clarissa Pinkola Estés for her profound insights; and my clients, all of whom have taught me so much.

Within the adoption reform movement, Florence Fisher who showed me the way in the beginning; Carole Andersen, Janet Fenton and Bonnie Bis of Concerned United Birthparents (CUB) for their constant enlightenment and guidance; Carol Schaefer and Rickie Solinger, for the contributions they have made and the one-two punch of energy, knowledge and healing that they gave at so many of my conferences; Don Humphrey and the Honorable Mary Smith for their tenacious fight for my right to my heritage; Bob Andersen and Rhonda Tucker for writing *The Bridge Less Traveled* and for their support; Gail Davenport for her steady presence as a friend; the late Jean Paton, the first adoptee with the courage to search and write about it a half century ago. Charlotte Hood for her faith in me. Sandy Musser for literally having the courage of her convictions. To my west coast connection, Karen, Mimi and Sharonfaith for being special moms in my life, to the late Emma May Vilardi who founded the International Soundex Reunion Registry, her husband Tony for carrying on her dream, Carol F or C from CT or PA for just being there, Celeste for her unsung help at conferences and finally to DeeAnn Macomson (and her Aunt Edith), who worked side-by-side with me for many years in my office.

For their dedication to adoption reform, my special "March Family," those who shared with me the six yearly walks from New York City to Washington, D.C., trekking down 250 miles of highway together in 100 degree heat, rain and exhaust fumes, in an effort to make the adoption world a better place for those touched by adoption: Ann C., her husband Martin and their son Charlie (in utero); Ann H.; Anna & her sons Avhram & Franklin; Barbara; Becky; Bob; Celeste & her son Scotty; DeeAnn; Desireé; Don; Geralynn; Ginger; Joyce; Judy & Dave; Kathy; Kristin; Laura & her children Brian, Katie and Suzie; Leah; Lisa & her mom Corinne; Marge; Marilyn; Mark; Mia; Michelle; Nancy C; Nancy H. & her daughter Shayna, Sarah, Shannon; Sue and finally Viney.

For composing the beautiful song *I Wonder Who My Mother Is?* for me to sing and record, I am grateful to the prolific and incomparable American song-writer Gladys Shelley.

If it weren't for the award-winning author of *Where are My Birthparents*, Karen Gravelle who suggested I write this book in the first place and whose words are part of this text with my own, there wouldn't be a book. To Darlene Gerow for her contribution of *Loss in the Adoption Hand-off*. For her editorial assistance in writing this book, and for her contributions to the adoption world, Jane Guttman. With gratitude to my publisher, Ann Hege Hughes, for her many years of encouragement and unending support.

Special thanks to Julie Goldman who stood by me through thick and thicker in my struggle to accomplish my goals and create this work.

Preface

---

*"They always say time changes
things, but you actually have to
change them yourself."* – Andy Warhol

As I lecture around the country, in book stores, libraries, social service agencies and other facilities, I am often told, usually angrily, by one or more of the attendees that I have broken their bubble, destroyed their dream.

"What bubble have I broken or dream destroyed?" I ask.

" That my child will be happy and have no pain. I didn't want to know what you have told me and I don't want it to be so!"

This book is about the realities of adoption and the realities of the inner world of the adopted person, from the beginning of her life. This book is not meant to blame. This book is to help future generations learn how to better treat children who cannot be raised by their original families.

Much of what I write I have learned from the vast knowledge and wisdom of my mentors and colleagues. Also, a great deal of what I write comes from 18 years of empirical research, working with adopted children, adolescents and adults, natural parents and adoptive parents.

I am not happy about what I have written here, but it needed to be written. It needs to be recognized as knowledge that can help heal those already hurt and help prevent some of the hurt for those who may become involved in or impacted by adoption. I am writing this book as an adoptee talking from the heart to his millions of adopted "brothers and sisters," as a son to millions of his natural parents and adoptive parents and as a colleague to his fellow mental health professionals.

I hope this gift can be accepted and ultimately unwrapped for use.

JS, New York, NY January 2000

Prologue:

The Politics of Adoption

Throughout most of our country's history, there have been more children who were without families and needing homes than families willing to adopt them. Even in the mid-1900s, when few children were actually orphaned, there generally were enough "illegitimate" births to provide a child to couples desiring to adopt.

In the 1970s, however, several events occurred that changed this picture dramatically, at least within the white population. With the availability of legal abortions, the number of white illegitimate births dropped precipitously. Other factors further reduced the supply of healthy white infants available for adoption. Illegitimacy became less of a stigma and unmarried mothers who kept their babies were no longer always social pariahs or unable to eventually find husbands. With the increased divorce rate among married couples and the subsequent impoverishment of divorced women and their children, the economic status of an unwed woman with a child began to resemble that of many families that had originated in wedlock. Additionally, as more and more marriages ended in divorce, other types of family organization besides the two-parent family began to receive acceptance as valid.

As a result of these changes, the argument that children born out of wedlock were better off being raised by a married couple than by an unwed natural parent had been seriously undermined. On the contrary, as discussed in *Adoption Healing*, evidence now indicates that at least a substantial segment of adoptees suffer long-lasting psychological damage as a result of having been separated from their natural mothers and severed from their genetic roots.

Coinciding with the dwindling supply of white infants available for adoption has been an explosion in the number of white couples who want to adopt. Several factors – including the trend toward postponing child bearing until the 30s and an increased incidence of sexually transmitted diseases such as chlamydia – have resulted in an increased infertility rate among white middle class couples, the group from which adoptive parents have traditionally come. While some of these individuals have benefitted from the new advances in infertility medicine, there remain many more couples eager to adopt white infants than there are children available to be adopted.

As the ads in newspapers throughout the country illustrate, potential adoptive parents have been reduced to placing ads in magazines, newspapers or other mass media to advertise themselves as dream couples in the hope of enticing an unwed mother to chose them to adopt her child. Unwed mothers, on the other hand, are increasingly demanding an "open adoption" as a condition of surrendering a child. Not surprisingly, most potential adoptive parents would like to avoid this arrangement if possible. Infertile couples generally want to create a family that resembles as closely as possible the "natural" family they are unable to have. This desire to resemble a non-adoptive family does not include recurrent reminders of their infertility or sharing their adopted child's love and loyalties with someone outside their own family. Even adoptive parents who are convinced of the benefits to the child of open adoption understandably approach this uncharted ground with trepidation. Finally, as the search/reunion movement gains momentum, parents who have managed to acquire a child must now deal with the continuing anxiety that the adoption may never be "final."

The conflicting needs of natural parents and their babies, on the one hand, and adoptive parents, on the other, has led to an alarming polarization of positions. This state of affairs is most dramatically illustrated in two bills that were recently before the New York State Assembly. One, sponsored by the Governor's wife, called for the opening of adoption records. At the same time, the other bill, which had at least the nominal support of the Governor, mandated sealed records. On the national level, the growing political pressure applied by the search/reunion groups to open all adoption records is being countered by legislation proposed by the National Conference of Commissioners on Uniform State Law. If enacted, this legislation would close all records for 99 years, and make those who divulge information – even when all parties involved consent to the disclosure – subject to imprisonment.

Unfortunately, in this climate, there is no middle position. While the purpose of *Adoption Healing* is to help heal wounds and facilitate healthier adoptions, the author firmly supports the opening of adoption records to all parties involved, supporting reunions between adoptees and natural parents and, whenever possible, keeping children within their families of origin from birth. As such, *Adoption Healing* is bound to generate controversy.

Proceed Gently

In the following pages, I will offer exercises, visualizations and affirmations. *If you are currently in therapy, please get your therapist's approval before starting these exercises, visualizations and affirmations.* You can do it by yourself using your adult self as a wise and caring person, but you still need your therapist's approval. In some of the exercises, your adult self will nurture your wounded inner child. You can do the exercises alone, but it would be better, at least in the beginning, for you to do them with a nurturing and supportive friend or even better with a support group.

These exercises are not intended to replace any therapy or therapy group that you may be involved in. They are not designed to replace any 12 step group that you might belong to. In fact they should enhance your therapy or 12 step work. **If you are an adult victim of sexual abuse or severe emotional battering,** or if you have been diagnosed as **mentally ill** or have a **history of mental illness** in either of your families, **professional help is essential for you.** If, as you read this book or experience these exercises, you start to *experience strange or overwhelming emotions, STOP IMMEDIATELY. PUT DOWN THE BOOK.* Obtain the help of a qualified counselor before you proceed. (The above cautions are substantially taken from *The Homecoming* by John Bradshaw)

Introduction

"Your mother loved you so much that she gave you away."
"Your real mother couldn't keep you/I'm your real mother."

Imagine what it's like to grow up hearing these mixed messages. For six million adoptees in the U.S. alone, they are a pervasive, *and fiercely debilitating,* fact of childhood. Their long-term impact is an existential catch-22 in which adoptees are forced to choose between the socially unacceptable reality they experience and a distorted, but socially sanctioned, interpretation of their reality as determined by others.

Based on 18 years of daily empirical research with literally thousands of adoptees, (children, adolescents and adults) *Adoption Healing* explores the crippling effect of this dilemma on adoptees' attempts to develop a healthy, authentic psychological and social sense of self. The ideas and theories expressed in this book are the result of the research, extensive readings, seminars and conversations with other adoption educators/mental health professionals.

From infancy, adoptees are bombarded by verbal and non-verbal messages from the outer world that directly negate and contradict their inner feelings and experiences. They are expected to be happy on their birthday, often the anniversary of their separation from their natural mother. They

> "Warding off early pain leads to amnesia about one's childhood... The thread to the child one once was is broken, leaving no trace of past experiences. Consequently, the wounded person is unable to experience her own feelings because her capacity to feel is no longer available to her." – *The Abandoned Child Within* – Kathryn Asper

are told that their natural mother loved them so much that she gave them away – a statement that must certainly leave them wondering about the desirability of being loved, to say nothing of the motives of their mother. They are given to understand both that their real mother gave them away and that their adoptive mother is their real mother. Most damaging of all, they are assured by the rest of us that they felt and continue to feel no sense of loss, no rage at having been abandoned.

Caught between these conflicting messages, adoptees are stuck in an emotional limbo, unable to accept either their inner, private reality or the fictional reality presented by those around them. Instead of an integrated whole, the adoptee's sense of self splinters, or *fractures,* into separate pieces. Since adoptees must function in

> "Though her soul requires seeing, the culture around her requires sightlessness. Though her soul wishes to speak its truth, she is pressured to be silent. Neither the child's soul nor her psyche can accommodate this." – *Women Who Run With the Wolves* – Clarissa Pinkola Estés

the outer world if they are to survive, their inner world can become increasingly repressed, eventually slipping out of reach. Survival is purchased at a heavy price, however, for without access to their inner feelings, adoptees are unable to live authentic lives.

Adoption Healing has been written in an attempt to provide adoptees, adoptive parents, and natural parents with knowledge and tools that can be used in healing this *fracture*. Vignettes from the lives of actual adoptees are presented throughout the book to illustrate the real-life manifestations of adoption-related problems and the successful growth and healing possible when these issues are understood and tackled correctly.

More than fifty thousand children are adopted into non-kinship American families each year. Since the 1970s, an increasing number of these adoptions have involved the placement of children with

> "Wow, there really was a woman who gave birth to me!" Marc, adoptee, age 37, upon learning the name of his natural

families from a different cultural and/or racial group. The special problems of these adoptions are addressed throughout the book.

Adoption is a family issue; thus, its effects extend far beyond the triad of adoptee, adoptive parents and natural parents. For this reason, *Adoption Healing* has much to offer the many others – siblings, spouses, grandparents, and children of adoptees – who are also struggling to cope with the impact of adoption.

This book is intended for both professional psychotherapists and the general public. While it would not be possible to bridge these two audiences in writing about most subjects, the nascent field of adoption psychology is an exception in that professional and lay groups overlap. Unlike other areas of psychology, in which professionals have led the way, the thinking expressed in this book has been generated to a significant degree by the efforts of adoptees and natural mothers to understand and define their own experience. Arising in large part from the grassroots search/reunion movement, the field of adoption psychology is therefore unique in the degree to which lay people have contributed to the development of psychological theory. In recognition of this, *Adoption Healing* is directed to all the "therapists" in adoptees' lives – professional counselors, adoptive parents, natural parents, spouses and family members, and, finally, adoptees themselves

This book is an attempt to educate, an attempt to understand one of the most misunderstood subjects in the world. This book is not about finger pointing. It *is* about learning from our mistakes so that we can perhaps reduce suffering in the future, especially for those who are separated from their children and mothers and fathers and sisters and brothers.

Welcome

Congratulations! You've made it to this page which is no small accomplishment. Adoption is a terror topic for most of us (unconscious as that fear might be.) It can be a very scary subject indeed. You have overcome much fear and anxiety just to open this book and now the real work begins. Let us continue with a visit to an adoption support group meeting. It is my hope that all of you will attend meetings such as this on a regular basis. The introduction to a typical support group meeting for those who have been separated by adoption goes like this:

Welcome to our support group meeting, especially those who are here for the first time. I would like to explain why we run the meeting the way we do and how to get the most out of it. Most of us grow up as adopted people (and for natural parents from the moment of surrender on) not allowed to express feelings about the experience. We may have been told not to be angry or that we weren't sad or that these feelings were not permitted. We were told we *should* not feel these feelings. Unfortunately, these messages do not work well. Feelings cannot be right or wrong. They just are! We need to be able to say what we feel to validate our experience. There are no *shoulds* when it comes to feelings. Can you imagine someone telling you that you are not allowed to say or *should* not say that it is cold outside or that saying you are hungry is not permitted?

The most difficult task we face is learning the language of our experience. We need to learn how to say, "I feel... (plug in: glad, sad, mad, ashamed, hurt, afraid, etc.) because... (fill in the blank in terms of your adoption experience.) When we say things out loud, they become real in a way they can never be if left unspoken; and when they become real, we can start to understand why we feel what we feel; and when we understand why, we can start to change the way that our experience affects us. We can begin the process of not being afraid of our feelings. We can learn that our feelings will not kill us, although it often feels like they can. When we become unafraid of our feelings, the world changes. Imagine being unafraid of your feelings!

What a glorious day that will be. This can happen for you, and by opening this book, you have just begun the journey toward wholeness by starting your adoption healing. The way we think about things has a great deal to do with how we experience them, as the example below shows very dramatically. A large portion of this book is about looking at things differently ("reframing" in shrink parlance) to change their effect on us and ultimately to understand that we actually can control how things affect us and how we feel. No one can make us feel anything. Contrary to what we were taught, no one is responsible for our feelings as adults and we are not responsible for the feelings of others. *What?* That's right. You are responsible for what you feel. I can say ugly words to you but you are responsible

> Imagine that you wake up in the middle of the night with a most terrible pain in the right side of your abdomen. You might well be terrified that the pain is the signal of the beginning of the end, an indication that your appendix is going to burst or that you have inoperable cancer. So you go to the doctor and he says that it's indigestion and tells you to take some Maalox. The pain will not change but your experience of it will. You will be unafraid of your pain and it will be perceived very differently.

for your reaction to them. This is an important concept and key to doing your healing. **How we think about things can change how we feel about them!**

Let us now continue on our journey. You should know that it is okay to put this book down from time to time, perhaps to process what you have read, perhaps to take a break from the highly emotional content. You should also know that only the truly brave and strong will read this book, so take the compliment! Only the brave and strong face their demons and that's what you are doing by reading this book.

As long as you are reading this book, it would be a good idea to start a journal now. Write your thoughts and feelings down as you progress on your journey toward healing and wholeness.

Part One:

The Missing Self

The disruptive impact of surrender on the psychological development of the adoptee

For reasons discussed at length in *Adoption Healing*, adoptees face special problems in negotiating each of the developmental stages of psychosocial development. The function of Part One is to help adoptees, adoptive parents, natural parents, and mental health professionals recognize the life-long impact of adoption and understand the ways in which adoption-related difficulties can interfere with the adoptee's personality development.

Although intended in part to provide an in-depth theoretical framework for mental health professionals, the material in Part One will be of even more immediate value to adoptees and their families. By articulating and explaining the forces that shape and psychologically *fracture* adoptees' personalities, Part One not only helps to validate their experience but provides them with a basis for beginning to deal with the difficulties they face in living full and authentic lives.

Chapter 1:

Genesis

The difficulties of the adoptee begin with the crisis faced by a resourceless pregnant woman, on the one hand, and the adoptive parents, on the other. Both sets of parents experience emotional trauma along with the decision to surrender/adopt, focusing in particular on unresolved problems that will continue to impact their lives and the life of the adoptee.

The importance of the adoptive parents' psychological state on the adoptee's development is easy to understand, since they are the ones who actually parent the child. It may be harder to appreciate the impact of the natural mother's unresolved emotional problems because it is usually assumed that she will have no further contact with the child. Her experience needs to be understood for a number of reasons, however. First is the simple concern for her as a human being. Secondly, much of the dishonesty surrounding adoption in the United States begins with the dismissal of her reality (and the misrepresentation of the realities of adoption to potential adoptive parents). Moreover, it is the firm belief of the author that an eventual reunion between the adoptee and natural mother is a major step in healing the wounds of surrender/adoption, and the natural mother's unresolved issues will certainly affect her ability to respond constructively to the adoptee at that point.

Finally, even if their paths never cross, the ghosts of the natural parents are always present in the adoptive family, and the ghosts of the child and the adoptive parents are always present in the birth family. These ghosts affect the lives of all concerned.

> The ghosts of the natural parents are the images and thoughts of the natural parents that are held in the minds of all those in the adoptive home.

Myths:

* When there is an adoption, everyone wins.
* Natural parents are just reproduction machines.
* Natural parents do not care about the babies they surrender to adoption.
* Natural parents soon forget the child they gave birth to and go on with their lives.

Facts:

* Everyone involved in an adoption has many losses.
* Natural parents are human beings just like everyone else.
* Most people surrender a child to adoption because they lack the resources to do otherwise.
* Natural parents care forever and have great difficulty going on with their lives.

In the beginning... there were a woman and a man who had a relationship including sex. When a pregnancy resulted, all their resources told them that if they really loved their baby, they should surrender her to adoption so she could have a better life. It would be unusual, even today, for someone to suggest that keeping the child might be best for them and their child. (Natural parent is a term used to described a parent who has surrendered a child to adoption, not someone who is pregnant.)

There is a couple who for years have been trying to have a baby and cannot. They suffer enormous pain and many indignities going through different procedures to "cure" their infertility. They may be advised to "adopt a baby and solve their problem that way." It would be unusual, even today, for someone to suggest that adopting a baby will *not* cure their infertility.

The pregnant woman and her partner are led to believe it is best for all concerned to surrender the baby to adoption. They are made to feel that they would be inadequate at best as parents, and incapable of giving the baby what she needs. The infertile couple are led to believe that they will be doing the baby and her parents a favor by "rescuing" her into their family.

> "...to give moral support to the ordinary good mother, educated or uneducated, clever or limited, rich or poor, and to protect her from everyone and everything that gets between her baby and herself." – *Home is Where We Start From* – DW Winnicott

For someone to be incapable of creating a child is an enormous wound to one's self. If one is going to adopt a child, attention should be paid to the wound of childlessness before embarking on alternative methods of parenting. Adoption is not a cure for infertility nor is it a way of erasing the sorrow and loss of self-esteem in not being able to reproduce. To parent well, one must fully deal with and mourn the loss of fertility. One must also recognize that raising an adopted child is not the same as raising a birth child and that an adoptive family is not the same as a birth family.

Both the pregnant couple and the prospective adoptive parents need to be informed that adoption is a *life-long* process and that all those involved will have pain associated with the adoption.

All involved need to be fully informed about the consequences on both sets of parents, but most important, on the effects of the loss of the mother-child relationship on the child. Adoption must be about the best interest of the child.

The adoptive parents must be aware that adoptive parenting *is* different and that adopted children have unique needs that must be met. The new parents must be aware that openness and honesty are of paramount importance in any family and that the adopted child must be dealt with truthfully. It is important to bear in mind that the ghosts of the natural parents will reside in the adoptive home and the ghosts of the adoptive parents and the baby will reside in the natural parents' homes. These ghosts affect the lives of all concerned. All involved are best served by having frequent communication and visitation between *all* parties to the adoption.

As you continue to read this book, I hope you will see that whenever possible, babies should remain within their family of origin or their extended family, and that the separation of a child from her original family is always detrimental to both. Yet, sadly, there will always be children who cannot be parented by their birth family members and it is my hope that these pages will help change the way adoptees are raised so that their lives are made easier and less painful along the way.

To Summarize

- Everyone involved in an adoption must understand completely the consequences of their decisions.
- Adoption is for babies who need parents, not for parents who want babies.
- A woman cannot simply forget a child she gives birth to.
- A woman cannot completely mourn the loss of her child to adoption. The pain will always be there.

Exercise

- Close your eyes and try to imagine what it would be like if your newborn baby was kidnapped while you were shopping. The loss of a child to adoption is no less painful or tragic.

Experience of the Moment

- You might be experiencing some tightness in your chest or some anxiety or pain. You might be feeling something undefinable. The emotions attached to our adoption experience are among the most powerful in human experience and need to be respected. It's okay to feel these things. Look around you. Reassure yourself that nothing is happening now. Say aloud in your head, "Nothing is happening now; I know it feels like it, but we are okay!" Memorize this because this is one of the most common and powerful of the healing affirmations that you will be learning as you progress on your journey. [What you just did was inner child work and what you said out loud in your head was an anti-anxiety affirmation.] Try to write down your feelings and thoughts in your journal.

Chapter 2:

The Primal Wound:
The First Trauma

Infants born prematurely and placed in incubators suffer noticeably from the loss of contact with their mothers. Although surrounded by nurses dedicated to giving them loving care, the infants obviously benefit from their mother's attention – even if that attention is filtered through sterile gloves and a mask. Yet a newborn separated from her mother and thrust into the arms of an adoptive mother is assumed to feel nothing.

Bonding occurs between a mother and her child before, during, and immediately after birth. A deep, primal wound is inflicted on the infant when this bond is abruptly and prematurely severed. As supported by recent research, newborns do not make the transition from natural mother to adoptive mother easily and naturally. On the contrary, adopted newborns know that

Bonding, a uniting force, is the formation of a deep emotional and physical connection between mother and child and is critical for the well being of the fetus and later the infant. Bonding provides, among other things, the ability for the fetus/infant to feel safe and secure. For a mother, the psychological bond with her child can begin with the contemplation of becoming pregnant, or anytime thereafter.

something is wrong, that someone is missing, and respond with sorrow and rage. This may result in the infant's withdrawal, lack of responsiveness, or subtle rejection of the adoptive parents.

The primal wound causes a fault line that is subject to varying underlying emotions, pressures that ultimately lead to the fracture or fragmenting of the personality that is more fully described in Chapter 5. Recognition of the primal wound requires natural mothers, adoptive parents, and adoptees to acknowledge that a tremendous injury has been inflicted on the adoptee. Because of the painful feelings this evokes in everyone concerned, most people involved resist acknowledging this damage. As the underlying basis of the problems adoptees face in constructing a self, however, the primal wound must be accepted as real and its effects understood before the resulting injury can be healed.

Myths:

*   Bonding begins after birth.
*   The infant does not experience her separation from her mother.
*   The infant is not affected by the loss of her original mother.
*   The adoptive family is the only family the adoptee has ever known.

Facts:

*   Bonding begins before birth.
*   The child experiences the separation from her mother.
*   The pain and anger of the separation are not forgotten.
*   The adoptee had a real relationship with her natural mother.

For a mother, bonding can begin before conception. For a child, bonding begins well before birth. By the end of the third trimester, this psychological and physical bond is well developed.

The fetus has memorized her mother's heartbeat and respiration, both sounds and rhythms; has memorized her mother's voice and her diurnal rhythm and immediately after birth, her smell. She can pick her face out of a line-up on the first day of life. If she is taken from her natural mother, she experiences the separation as painful and anger

> "There is no such thing as an infant, only the mother-infant system... It is dreadful to not know whether something is fact, or mystery or fantasy." – *The Theory of Parent Infant Relationships* – DW Winnicott

provoking. (Think of the infant who is removed from the breast or bottle before she is ready: Her cheeks turn bright red, she balls up her little fists and howls with rage and unmet needs.) This most important bond is broken when a child is separated from her mother. This is the "Primal Wound,"[2] and what I believe is the first of many traumas.

The infant *should* now be treated as a survivor of a trauma. She has just suffered the psychological death of her mother and should be treated accordingly. (It should be noted that the infant's mother has also just suffered the psychological death of her child.) This trauma very often causes hyper-vigilance, an extreme state of wariness in the infant/child. The hyper-vigilance, which is really watching for psychological danger, can continue on into adulthood and frequently causes panic attacks. It feels like "It" is happening again. "It," the separation from one's mother, is what the adoptee fears most, and the most subtle, perhaps unnoticeable event or trigger can cause a very extreme reaction at any age.[3]

The "mother-child" relationship is irreplaceable. The separation is an unresolvable loss for both, a loss that should be avoided if at all possible. Your mother of birth can give you

---

[2] Nancy Newton Verrier, M..A., *The Primal Wound*

[3] Judith Hermann, *Trauma and Recovery*

something that no other person can.[4] Immediately following birth, If there is no separation of mother and child, this most sacred of relationships continues. The newborn is returned to her mother's breast, and once again she hears her heartbeat and respiration, smells the familiar smell and gazes intently into her eyes, apparently receiving some special comfort from them. Skin to skin contact along with the familiar smell, voice and eyes activates the baby's nerve endings and shuts off the stress hormones that were activated at birth. Without this skin to skin contact, the baby's adrenaline keeps flowing and you have a "hyper" baby. The bonding that began before birth continues. Her mother is emotionally and physiologically primed to nurture, and hormones and instincts are racing through her body.   The newborn is emotionally and physiologically primed to be nurtured by *her* mother. The newborn will basically remain as one (both physically and psychologically) with her mother for about nine months, gradually coming to realize that she is a separate entity at the end of that period of time, and developing a natural boundary of separateness.

When there is a premature separation, the infant experiences being taken from everything safe in the world to a place of strangers (well intentioned to be sure) where nothing feels safe, nothing feels right, sounds right or looks right. The adoptive mother doesn't even smell right! Whether or not you agree that an infant can recognize her mother by her individual smell, adoptive mothers do not smell like lactating women. They also don't move like a woman who has just given birth. New

> "The horrors of war pale beside the loss of a mother" – Anna Freud "and the loss of a baby" - Joe Soll

mothers are readjusting to their new bodies and move very differently from women who haven't just gone through the changes of pregnancy and birth. A separated infant may push the "wrong" mother away, and adoptive mothers may misinterpret this gesture. As the child becomes older, she may not want hugs from adoptive

---

[4] Hope Edelman, *Motherless Daughters*

parents for this reason and a variety of others.

Compounding this problem, adoptive mothers are often tentative mothers. They are often insecure about holding a newborn. This insecurity may stem from an unconscious belief that they may not be capable as a parent if they were not capable of bringing a child into this world. An infant will sense this and perhaps react with rigidity, seemingly not wanting affection, when that is not the case at all. Infants "know" everything. They are receptors of feelings. If a parent is angry or sad or tense or frightened, the newborn will sense this and react with anxiety or fear herself.

When there is a separation, an artificial boundary is formed between infant and mother and then in the adoptive home, the adoptive mother (understandably) tries to remove that so that she can "bond" with what is now "her" child. Unfortunately, bonding can only occur with one's natural mother. However, strong and healthy attachments can be made with one's adoptive family. Adoptive families

> "A healthy boundary is an internalized limit, physical, emotional, intellectual, spiritual that enhances a sense of identity by implanting more deeply the precious knowledge that one is a separate human being" – *Living in the Comfort Zone* – Rokelle Lerner

often have very loose boundaries partly because they want the adopted child to be like them, think like them, do like them, making it harder for the adoptive parents to recognize the adoptee's unique and inherent self.

Adoption has been looked at as a cure for infertility. If it is looked at that way, the parents will pretend everything is "as if." There is a strong investment on all sides to pretend, to act "as if" the adoptee was born into the family. The adoptee often strives to act like and be like and do like her adoptive parents, however, "as if" just doesn't work. Every time, for example, an adoptee hears the statement, "I love you as if you are my own," it's a slap in the face.

No one can love someone "as if" they were someone else. Saying to your child, "I love you very much" will do nicely.

Pretending everything is "as if" is a wonderful way to stay away from conscious pain and promote an unhealthy atmosphere. Pretending will lead you to have the "dead horse on the dining room table" and many families never acknowledge that adoption is an issue that is "smelling up" the family relationship, keeping the family members from dealing with reality. The "dead horse" is a metaphor for a fact that everyone knows but no one will acknowledge... the adoption. Not acknowledging the "dead horse" of adoption is a way of keeping a secret and secrets are poison to all relationships. Keeping the secret creates tension in the home and children always react in a negative way to tension, feeling unsafe, worrying about the cause of the tension and perhaps, because children see the world as revolving around them, blaming themselves.

It is still believed in many circles that adoptees come with a blank slate and can become whatever the adoptive parents wish. However, every child is born with genetic traits such as temperament and talents as part of their makeup, things that cannot be changed. Adoptees will often subdue (unconsciously) their natural way of being to make their adoptive parents happy. Since the one thing that an adoptee does not want to happen again is to lose another family, the adoptee often becomes a "people pleaser" extraordinaire. She sacrifices herself to keep her parents happy (and thereby insuring her remaining in her home.)

> "Emotional abandonment of the child creates uncertainty about her feelings... whether she ought to be having them, and even what they are. This continues into adulthood, leading to a sense of not having the 'right' to feel. In other words, she has stopped feeling, and can no longer even perceive her own feelings." – Kathryn Asper

Infertility is a very painful wound that needs to be addressed. If this wound is not dealt with and family pretends that the adoption cured the infertility, then the adoptee becomes the fixer whose job is to keep her parents from having the pain of infertility. What a formidable task for any infant! The adoptee may keep the role of fixer and people pleaser for her entire life. And what a price she pays!

To Summarize

- The mother-child relationship is sacred and the separation of mother and child is a tragedy for both.
- The separation is a primal wound and the first of many traumas.
- The losses must be recognized and not hidden.
- All those involved in adoption must treat each other and their losses with great respect.

Exercise

- Close your eyes and try to imagine what it would be like if you were told that your mother had died when you were born. The loss of a mother is painful and tragic no matter how or why it happens.

Experience of the Moment

- You might be feeling unsafe right now. After all, if you are adopted, you just read about the loss of your mother. We will often re-experience the loss of our mothers and the experience can be very frightening. You might also be angry about what happened to you and/or your mother. That is all right too. There is nothing wrong with being angry. You might be frightened of your anger or your pain or your sadness. These are only feelings, powerful yes, but only feelings. Repeat the affirmation from Chapter One. Say aloud in your head, "Nothing is happening now; I know it feels like it, but we are okay!" It may sometimes feel like you will cry and never stop, or you will disintegrate, or explode.

It may feel like that, but those are only feelings. If you still feel unsafe, repeat the affirmation and if you need to, call a friend for support. Bear in mind that you can always put this book down. It is important for you to be aware that you are an expert at hiding from these feelings. We all are. So you can put up a wall against these feelings anytime you wish. That's okay too. Try to write down your feelings and thoughts in your journal.

Chapter 3:

Age of Discovery:
The Second Trauma

Somewhere around age two or three, adoptees are told – usually by the adoptive parents – that they are adopted. Contrary to conventional wisdom, this is *not* when adoptees first learn that they had a prior mother. As Nancy Verrier says in the, *Primal Wound*, "Remember, [the adoptee] was there [at the birth and separation]!" The verbalization of this fact is, however, the first conscious confirmation of what is already known and has considerable impact on the child's development. Although telling the child that she is adopted confirms what is already known, the way in which parents convey this information will greatly influence the child's response to the conscious knowledge of adoption.

"The child separated from her mother at or soon after birth misses the mutual and deeply satisfying mother-child relationship, the roots of which lie in that deep area of personality where the physiological and psychological are merged. This is part of a biological sequence... It is doubtful whether the relationship of the child to its post-partum mother, in its subtler effects, can be replaced by even the best of substitute mothers. The infant is traumatized by its separation from the mother at birth." – *The Psychology of the Adopted Child* – Florence Clothier

Myths:

*   Telling the adopted child a "good" story will eliminate pain.
*   The adopted child has no idea that anything "happened" at the beginning of her life.
*   The child will not understand what you are telling her.

Facts:

*   There is no story that you can tell an adopted child that will eliminate pain.
*   The discovery of her adoptive status is a conscious confirmation of what is already known to the child.
*   The adopted child will feel sadness and pain at the disclosure.

There are those who would say that an adopted child should never be told she is adopted. Others would say don't tell the child until she is 'older' and can understand. There are many reasons why the above beliefs are misguided.

1)   First and foremost, the adopted child was there and experienced the separation from her mother. While the child has no words to describe the experience, because it was pre-verbal, the adopted child *knows* something happened. The traumatic feelings surrounding the separation may, unfortunately, recur often in the adoptee's life.

2)   The child *must* be told before she enters any kind of school. The risk of hearing the adoption story from another child is too high and can be especially traumatic.

3)   A child should *not* be told: that she came from an adoption agency; that her parents loved her so much that they gave her up; that her parent(s) died; that her parents did not love her; that she was abandoned or that she was brought by the stork.

4)   The child will emotionally understand that something profound has happened and very probably will show sadness, anger and confusion. Validate this for the child by acknowledging her feelings.

5)   It is far better if the child is told in a planned way rather than if the adoptive parents (particularly mom) are forced into a conversation when off guard. It is very likely that your child will ask at some particularly inconvenient time: "Did I come from your tummy, mommy?" The parents need to pick a time to sit down with their child and tell her about her adoption. It is very important that the adoptive parents have dealt with their pain about adoption. If they have not, their child will sense their pain and that will cause the child to cease to talk about her own pain.

6)   Nothing can make the loss of a mother "all right."

7)   If the adopted child shows sadness or anger or pain, validate it! Let the child know that feeling the anger, sadness or pain is understandable. This is validating her feelings. The adopted child has good reason for these feelings and must not be left to deal with them alone.

8)   The feelings from the second trauma will accumulate on top of the feelings from the first trauma, adding to the depth of pain anger and sadness that the adopted child must carry internally.

9)   The adopted child must be treated as if her natural mother actually died.

10)   Adoptive parents should reinforce their love and caring and their sadness that their child had to experience this loss. Let the adopted child be the guide.

To Summarize

- The adopted child has just been told that her mother "died."
- The child experiences this as a very devastating loss.
- No one can make this all right.
- The adoptive child will need a lot of TLC.
- The adoptive parents' feelings surrounding their infertility. must be dealt with for them to effectively deal with their child's feelings.

Exercise

- Close your eyes and try to picture that young child just having been told that she has another mother out there that gave birth to her. What do you suppose she is feeling? What would help comfort her? Try to imagine being that child and being held and comforted by your natural mother. Hear her say "I love you" and "it is sad that I cannot be with you now." Understand that this child is in great distress. Help make this child feel safe. Tell her that it is okay to feel any feeling she has.

Experience of the Moment

- You might start to feel unsafe. It is important to understand that the experience of the loss of a mother at birth can only happen one time. The child can never experience it again.

If you are adopted, say out loud in your head, "I know it may feel like it is happening now, but it is *not* and it can never happen again. You are safe." Look around you to make sure this is so. Remember that any feelings you might be having are normal. Scary yes, but normal. Try to write down your feelings and thoughts in your journal.

Chapter 4:

Oedipus Wrecks

The *Oedipus complex*, in Freud's theory of child development, consists of the unconscious attraction developed by a young child (usually between ages 3 and 7) for the parent of the opposite sex while at the same time, the child would experience feelings of rivalry with the parent of the same sex. These unconscious feelings often manifest themselves in flirtatious behavior with the opposite sex parent and passive-aggressive behavior with the same sex parent. Passive-aggressive behavior is generally the unconscious expression of anger through actions rather than words.

Resolution of the Oedipal complex, a necessary step in the child's development, is complicated by the fact that adoptees have a phantom set of parents (the phantom or ghost parents are the ever-present thoughts and feelings about the natural parents) in addition to the adoptive parents

> Simply put, the resolution of the *Oedipal conflicts* would mean the cessation of the unconscious attraction for one's parents resulting in a healthy set of boundaries in relationship to one's parents.

with whom they live. The adopted child of this age will likely fantasize about similar unconscious feelings of attraction for the unknown natural parents. Thus, any resolution is only a partial one, since the feelings about the missing or ghost parents are never truly explored in a real way.

Children at this age will experience their mothers as either all good or all bad. This is called *splitting*. The *splitting* of the mother into all good or all bad is exacerbated for the adoptee by the existence of two actual mothers to take these roles of good and bad.

Myths:

- Adopted children don't think about their natural mothers.
- Adopted children have no conflicts about being adopted.
- Adopted children do not have any particular developmental problems.

Facts:

- Adopted children think about their natural mothers *all* the time.
- Adopted children have a conflict between two mothers that starts developing, at the very latest, when they discover they're adopted.
- Adopted children process their developmental milestones differently than non-adopted children.

The *Oedipal* conflicts of the child can be a very confusing time for parent and child alike. A child at this age is not capable of understanding that a mother is not all good or all bad depending on how she treats her child. From the child's perspective, if her mother is treating her well, she is a good mommy. If she withholds something the child wants, she is a bad mommy. Both natural and adoptive mothers are alternatively seen as good and

> "Where love once was or might have been is now blocked. The person ... moves in search of the lost mother of infancy." – *In Search of the Lost Mother of Infancy* – Lawrence E Hedges

bad at different times during this phase of development. Moreover, there is an unconscious internal conflict between the two mothers. From the young child's perspective, thinking too much about the mother that is not present may make the child believe that her thinking about her natural mother may cause the mother on the scene to leave her. Additionally, if she thinks too much about her adoptive mother, she might believe that her missing natural mother may stop caring about her.

Any fantasies that the child has about her adoptive mother will probably include fantasies about her natural mother as well. Whenever her adoptive mother does something she doesn't like, the child will probably view her as the bad mommy and think that her natural mother wouldn't treat her this way, because she is the good mommy. Conversely, there will be times when she envisions her natural mother as bad for giving her up, and her adoptive mommy as the good one.

Resolution of this conflict is complex and difficult to achieve. There is likely to be tremendous inner turmoil for the child and it can be very difficult for her to stop *splitting* with her adoptive mother as long as she has only the ghost of her natural mother to deal with. Special attention must be given to the adopted child during this period of her life, understanding that she may be having a very stressful experience.

It is very hard for the adopted child to have a consistently close relationship with her new mother when she has so many confused fantasies about both her mothers. The more the child can be helped to express her feelings about both mothers, and have her confusions explained to her, the easier her passage through this developmental stage.

To Summarize

- This is an important stage in a child's development.

- It is important to bear in mind that the adopted child is going through a very confusing and difficult time.
- Helping the adopted child talk about what she is experiencing will help her cope better with this confusing time of her life.
- Do not forget that the adopted child has suffered a loss and is in pain.

Exercise

- Close your eyes and try to see that young child in your mind. If you are an adoptee, step into the picture as the adult and talk out loud in your head to that young child. Ask her how she is feeling. Tell her that you are her, all grown up, and that you have come to help her. Be aware that she will need some time to trust you. She will always know what she needs from you to feel better. Listen to her. You will eventually hear her spontaneously respond to you. Establish a loving relationship with her.

Experience of the Moment

- It will feel weird initially to carry on these "inner child" conversations. You will know it is working when the response from the child is unexpected or spontaneous. You will not create the answers, she will. Giving your inner child what she asks for will have tremendous healing effects for her and for you the adult.

Chapter 5:

Fracturing:
The Third Trauma

Latency, the stage at which the adopted child's personality begins to fracture and a feeling of being in limbo begins, is perhaps the most critical point in the adoptee's psychosocial development. Confronted by a series of conflicting messages – "Your mother loved you so much that she gave you away; your real mother couldn't keep you/I'm your real mother; happy birthday/this is the day you were surrendered" – the adoptee is unable to integrate basic information about her

> **FRACTURING** is an acronym for the simultaneous feelings that the adopted child is surrounded by: Frustration, Rage, Anxiety, Confusion, Terror, Unrest, Regret, Inhuman, Neglected, Grief.

reality. Moreover, the child remembers these conflicting messages and hears them over and over again as if they were being played back by a tape recorder.

The child's response to this mental "running tape" of internalized messages from the outside world resembles the stages of dying – anger, denial, sadness, grieving, repression, shutting down emotionally, and (a false) acceptance of the situation. The child's and subsequently the adult's psychological underpinnings become based on false beliefs, widening the fault lines created from the primal wound, and the *fracture* then occurs. Behaviorally, many adoptees escape into day dreams and have difficulty concentrating, often **appearing** to have Attention Deficit Disorder or learning disabilities.

Not surprisingly, since they don't know what they did to cause their natural mothers to surrender them, adoptees frequently worry unconsciously they may do something that will prompt their adoptive parents to abandon them as well. The child tends to handle the anxiety this provokes in one of two ways – either by rebelling in an effort to force the other shoe to drop (being abandoned again) or, more frequently to avoid further abandonment, by attempting to be super-good, (being a perfect child) but always walking on an invisible tightrope, unconsciously trying to make sure not to repeat the original "mistake" and once again be rejected. From the parent's perspective, the fault lines seem to disappear and the fracture is hardly noticeable.

Myths:
- If the child looks okay (smiles etc.), the child is okay.
- The child feels lovable because the parents say so often.
- The adopted child is just like every other child.
- If the child has concerns about adoption, she will voice them.

Facts:
- Children quickly learn how to hide their negative feelings if they are not validated and once the feelings are hidden or repressed, which is an unconscious process, they are unaware of the existence of such feelings.

- The adopted child is unlikely to really believe she is loveable.

- Adopted children are different. Their mothers effectively "died" for them at birth and they are in pain.

- Children will often not talk about something their parents are afraid of.

During the ages of six to eight, there is a "window of opportunity" to reduce further trauma. This is the age when the child becomes cognitive, able to start logical thought. This age is the most likely time for the adopted child to start asking questions about her natural parents as she is thinking about adoption logically for the first time. This is the time, as she begins to play an internal tape about her own lovability, that

> "One of the greatest wounds a child can receive is the rejection of her authentic self. When a parent cannot affirm her child's feelings, needs and desires, she rejects the child's authentic self. Then, a false self must be set up." – *The Homecoming* – John Bradshaw

she may say that she wants her "real" mommy. As painful as it is for her parents to hear, it is important to understand that this is not about the present parents but about the loss of her natural parents.

After asking questions and/or thinking about what happened to her, it is inevitable that the child's running internal tape will be, "If she REALLY loved me she would have kept me. I must be defective and my defect is that I am not lovable." The child will now feel enormous pain, sadness and rage. If we can be aware of the child's dilemma during the playing of the "tape" we can encourage and assist the child in expressing her negative feelings about her lovability and feelings of rejection in order to help her understand that it is not her fault. If we do not help the child grieve this most sacred loss and express her rage and indignation, she will continue to play the tape and believe (unconsciously) that she is unlovable. This playing of the tape (and the resultant feelings of unlovability) is the third trauma and what I call the *fracturing* of her personality.

The personality now sits on fault lines on top of the fault lines of the *primal wound*. The psyche is on shaky ground and the child cannot cope with these feelings. The individual feelings of pain, anger and sadness get woven together into one enormous painful but indistinguishable emotion which you might call the "loss of mother" emotion. This "emotion" must be repressed for the child to survive. As a result, the child is likely to repress other parts of her childhood along with this interwoven "emotion" as she cannot repress the emotions without substantially losing some of the memories of this time of her life. The child may well think of it later in life as the "adoption loss emotion" or something similar. These feelings are now indistinguishable from each other so that anytime the child touches any of her emotions about her loss, she will touch the whole fabric of her emotions, which is too painful for her to cope with and she will have to shut down again.

Many adoptees will talk of adoption as a wonderful thing, but be unaware of these powerful negative emotions concerning the loss of their natural mother. The child has had to turn off. She may appear just fine, because that is the act she has to put on, both for her parents whom she does not wish to disappoint by being unhappy, (a failure on the child's part that may cause another abandonment) and for herself, so that she can continue to repress that big ball of emotion. She has now entered the state of "limbo."

Later in life, it will be very difficult for the adoptee to talk about her emotions because this fabric of tangled emotions is so painful and so difficult to unravel. We will talk about ways to accomplish this unraveling of emotions in Part Two of this book.

> It is interesting to note that natural mothers very often start to "wake up" after six to eight years of being numb. Perhaps this is in response to the impending fracture of her child, who will unfortunately have this fracturing experience between six to eight years of age.

At this stage, before the fracture and in an ideal world, it would be wonderful to have a reunion with the child and her original family. It would heal much of the child's wounds, and help prevent further trauma. I know that some say it would be too confusing for a child to have two mothers. However, the truth is, it is more confusing and painful to not know one's natural mother. We allow a child to see two mothers in divorce situations all the time. We need to do the same in adoption, have the adults act like adults and put the child first.

For the child, the state of "limbo" is a land of no reality. The mind is now overloaded with conflicting thoughts and stories. "Your real mother is the one who gave birth to you but she is not your real mother because she didn't keep you and I am not your real mother because I didn't give birth to you, but I am your real mother because I have you now." Effectively, this is the message that most adopted children get. Or, "Happy birthday, honey." "But mommy, I am sad" (anniversary reaction)... "No, you are not, you are happy". Or, "Mommy, I am angry"... "No, you have nothing to be angry about, you're so special. We are so glad we chose you. And you are so lucky." "Who do I look like mommy?"... Silence or, "Why honey, you look just like Aunt Jane."

The "state of limbo" is a never-never land between feeling and being psychologically dead. It feels as if coming out of "limbo" will kill. All of those emotions that were repressed at the time of the "fracture" lie in wait, unless diffused by outside help. Most adoptees feel as if they are unborn, not alive, that what happened is a dream, could not possibly be true. After all, how could you possibly be raised by someone other than your "real" mother. And for many, it is safer to stay in "limbo", then risk annihilation by daring to feel one's real feelings. If you pay close attention, adoptees often show no emotion or shallow emotion. That's what it is like to live in "limbo", no emotion and often, experiencing a psychological death.

Being in this "state of limbo" can last for the rest of the adoptee's life. If the adoptee decides to search or get some counseling, she can leave the "limbo" state by committing herself to the process of self-knowledge and change.

To Summarize

- The age of cognition is the time when an adoptee will play a tape in her head that says she is defective and the defect is unlovability. To her, this is proven by the fact that she was given away.

- Once the adoptee plays the tape and believes she is unlovable, she *fractures.* Her horribly painful emotions get twisted into a ball that is too big to handle and the emotions and the playing of the tape get repressed.

- The adoptee now enters the "land of limbo."

- There is a window of opportunity before the adoptee enters *limbo* to prevent it, or at the very least ameliorate the effects of the tape.

- Do not forget that the child is left alone to cope with these feelings. These same feelings are so powerful that adult adoptees most often initially feel incapable of surviving them, but with support and assistance, they *can* be overcome.

Exercise

- Close your eyes and see your inner child about the age of cognition (six to eight) and step into her space. Ask her how she is feeling. Ask her if she is sad, if she doesn't offer it. Tell her that it is okay to be sad and perhaps angry also. Observe her face. Ask her if she would like a hug and if so, give it to her. Tell her you love her, that she can trust you more than anyone else in the world and that you will never leave her. (You can't, can you?) Tell her again that it wasn't about her, that she is lovable. It wasn't her fault even though she feels that way sometimes, but you *know* it wasn't her fault. Give her another hug. Tell her you have to go do some errands, but that you are on 24 hour call and you will always respond to her. Give her another hug and another "I love you," and let yourself come back to the here and now.

Experience of the Moment

- You might be experiencing some sadness right now. This sadness is very likely to be from the losses that most people involved in adoption have suffered. Be respectful of your emotions and understand that you are feeling them because you need to and that it is normal.

Should you think that you are acting like a crybaby or feeling sorry for your self, or that you are weak for crying, understand that only strong people are willing to let themselves feel the pain of their losses. And it is not feeling sorry for your self to feel sad about a sad event. It's about time that you did let yourself feel sad. (Isn't it?)

If you start to feel unsafe or anxious that something bad is going to happen, address your inner child by saying out loud in your head, "Nothing is happening now, it only feels like it. Look around and see that this is so. We're okay."

Chapter 6:

The Wreck Revisited

Adoptees are handicapped in accomplishing virtually all the tasks of adolescence. Because they lack the basic knowledge of their biological roots, they have a harder time trying to form their own sense of identity. In addition, adoptees experience more difficulty in separating from their parents than do other teenagers, in part because they must cope with phantom parents as well as flesh and blood ones.

Finally, the issues of sexuality that all adolescents grapple with are, for adopted teenagers, inevitably intertwined with and complicated by the issue of their own origins and surrender. Their growing interest in sexual relationships stimulates questions about their own conception, thus increasing their anger. Adoptees at this age frequently search for their natural mothers unconsciously through boyfriends or girlfriends and, in an effort to identify with their natural mother, female adoptees all too frequently become pregnant. Male adoptees, on the other hand, tend to express their rage physically.

Myths:

- Teenagers act like teenagers and adopted adolescents are the same as everybody else.
- It does not matter if you don't know your roots, your heritage.
- You get your identity from your adopted parents.

Facts:

- Adolescent adoptees have their own set of specific problems that are very difficult to deal with unless help and support is available.
- If you don't know your true heritage, it creates enormous pain and difficulty, especially during adolescence.
- Your identity is tied to your past and your heritage.

Adolescence is a developmental stage when human beings (consciously or unconsciously), start to think about and desire the perfect set of parents who could have raised them. This "desire" is called the family romance fantasy. Hopefully at the end of this period, (often lasting into our twenties) we realize that our parents are fallible human beings who did the best they could (hopefully), loved us (hopefully), and that indeed, they were the only ones who could have parented us.

Adopted adolescents, however, **know** that another set of parents could have raised them. This can cause tremendous difficulty. The adopted individual is reminded of this each morning (at least) when she looks into

> The famous therapist, Erik Erikson, discovered that he was adopted when he was twenty years old. Erikson said that if you don't know your biological family, you cannot establish a sense of actuality. What he meant by actuality was the ability to connect to people and events in a real way.

the mirror and sees the face of a stranger because she has never seen anyone who looks like her. For the adoptee, the fantasy is a reality and so begins a new way of thinking about the natural parents. The questions: Who, What, Where, When, How and Why. These thoughts (again, conscious or unconscious) haunt the adoptee. Could that woman on the street be my mother? That man, could he be my father? Or that one, could she be my sibling? In reality this is torture. Adoptees therefore, have a great deal of difficulty accepting their adoptive parents as fallible human beings who did the best that they could. Or, conversely, the adoptee will come to view their adoptive parents as the perfect parents who did indeed raise them, thereby repressing the true conflict. These adoptees will often say, "I'm glad she gave me up," in a further attempt to deny their hidden feelings and the reality of their situation.

Adoptee's have identity gaps[5], brought about by incomplete information about their past. Adoptees know who they are (what their parents have said they are) and at the same time they don't. "My family is my family, but I have another family." How can the adoptee integrate two families into her identity when she only knows about one? There are more existential questions. Why did this happen to me? Did it really happen? What am I going to do with my life? The expression, "The future is blind without sight of the past" is so true for adopted persons. Adoptees have great difficulty deciding what road to travel in their lives. Should I be a.....? Adoptees often try one career, followed by another and another. Many adoptees, like non-adoptees, often stick with the first career, afraid to change, but it is often very unsatisfying. Many adoptees choose the career their parents want. The difficulty in part is that adoptees do not grow up surrounded with blood relatives whose talents they can see, whose careers they can consider as being truly a part of their nature. It is not that if their birth grandpa was a wood cutter that they would become a wood cutter, but they would get to think about it and reject

---

[5] Sorosky, Baran & Pannor, *The Adoption Triangle*

it if they wished. It is a part of who they are.

Perhaps most troubling of all is that if you are shut down and cannot feel your *real* feelings (due to the fracture), if you cannot know your innermost thoughts and feelings about yourself, your two mothers and your feelings about the world that "did" this to you, how can you make good decisions? You don't have enough information without these feelings. Adoptees think about the world differently than other people and their thought processes therefore often lead to decisions that don't work well.

Adolescent hormones are raging, and during this hectic and confusing time, adoptees think about their creation, about which they know little or nothing, and they question themselves. Who am I really? Often, there is gender confusion. If I don't know who I really am, maybe I am not really a man, or not really a woman. This is very painful and often increases their anger; Adoptees often search for their natural mother in their relationships with girlfriends and boyfriends, another avenue through which to reconnect with her. These relationships are often extremely intense and often resemble the relationship between a newborn and her mother. This behavior often continues throughout the life of the adoptee. Adoptees commonly choose their partners poorly (not being able to feel their real feelings and acting on the neediness of their inner child) and frequently pick people who are unavailable. If the adoptee does pick someone available, the adoptee will often sabotage the relationship. **Closeness can lead to being abandoned again**. Adoptees can have great difficulty having adult relationships with their partners because of the unmet needs of their childhoods.

When we can help the adoptee to get in touch with their real feelings, recognize the unmet needs of their infancy for what they really are, and understand that what happened at birth can never happen again, they can start to pick better and learn to have good loving adult relationships with their partners.

The expression of anger and sadness with behavior rather than words, or acting-out, by adoptees can be heightened during adolescence. Anger, pain and sadness are cumulative emotions. Events and thoughts that cause these emotions go into a pot that just gets more full with each experience. The adoptee has had three (at least) traumas and the pot is very full. If we do not help the adoptee express these emotions in a healthy way, the pot is ready to explode. Then, as happens too often for some, we walk into the deli and ask the deli-man for a corned beef on rye with mustard, he gives it to us with mayo and we want to tear him apart. This type of experience is typical of an adoptee. Not knowing how to express her rage, perhaps (commonly) not recognizing its existence, the pot is full and the slightest provocation puts the whole weight of the anger pot into the unrelated feelings of the moment.

In general, it takes real physical energy to keep secrets and keep the repressed emotions hidden. When we start to feel our hidden feelings such as anger etc., we free up the energy we were using to keep our feelings bottled up. We will have more energy to live our lives. We will feel much better, and **when we let ourselves feel our pain and anger and sadness and all of life's other feelings, we can then and only then feel true happiness!**

When we learn how to channel anger, we use its energy to do things and gain the benefit of having more good energy for enjoyment.

To Summarize

- Adoptees have a particularly difficult time during adolescence.
- The lack of information about their heritage exacerbates their difficulties.
- It's normal for adoptees to be in crisis during adolescence.
- When adoptees act-out, it is an expression of their pain and

confusion about their identity.

- Rage, pain and sadness are cumulative emotions and a very small annoying event can cause the adoptee to experience all of her anger from the past.

Exercise

- Write down in your journal, as best you can, all you can recall about this period in your life. What were you doing, feeling and thinking? How did you and your parents get along? You may remember a lot, or relatively little. That's okay. Close your eyes and try to visualize yourself as a teenager. Walk into the picture as before and ask your younger self what she is feeling. Listen for a spontaneous response. Try to carry out a dialogue with your younger self and write the dialogue down in your journal. Bear in mind that it takes time to be able to do this. It is not always easy to begin, but when you are able to do this easily, the rewards are great in terms of healing and feeling good about yourself.

Experience of the Moment

- You might start to feel angry. It is all right to feel angry. It's only a feeling. Anger is normal to feel; it is only what you do with it that is important. You might try to say out loud in your head, "I am going to take my anger and use it to paint a picture, write a story, run around the block, clean the house or do the dishes... "You fill in the blank. This is called channeling anger and it is a very effective way of reducing the anger that has accumulated within you. You can channel your anger into any non-sedentary activity, and aside from feeling better, you will not blow up as you have in the past. You don't have to feel your anger to channel it, just be aware that it is there. You discover that this gives you more energy to live your life. Can you imagine the relief of not having to hold in your feelings anymore?

Chapter 7:

Incomplete Crossing

Adoptees may face many problems in their early twenties, particularly in developing relationships and in choosing a career. They have tremendous difficulty trusting anyone in relationships, for many reasons. One could make the case that it would be very difficult for an adoptee to ever trust a woman, since it was a woman who left the adoptee in the beginning of her life. However, women have just as much difficulty in relationships with men as men do with women. If someone is gay or lesbian, they

> "People... who are narcissistically wounded not only have a poor connection to themselves, they also relate poorly to other people, especially when their loss occurred early. Because of such experiences, they mistrust other people, and each separation, regardless of how distant, evokes a fear that prevents them from entering into relationships." – *The Abandoned Child Within* – Kathryn Asper

may have additional problems with relationships. However, it doesn't matter what the sex of the adoptee is, adoptees usually have difficulty trusting others in any type of relationship. Similarly, they have a hard time choosing an educational focus and committing to career plans, because they often are not in touch with their wants and desires. This affects decisions with regard to both relationships and careers.

More than their non-adopted counterparts, adoptees are hindered in taking control of their lives by an internal struggle related to the conflict between their own wants and desires, the pressure and desire to please their adoptive parents, and the imagined hopes and dreams that their idealized natural mothers may have for them. The conflict between the two mothers comes into play at every stage of development. In the early stages of adulthood, this conflict plays a significant role in the development of long-term relationships, as adoptees may search for partners based on their imagined relationships with their natural mother, while reacting to their current relationships with their adopted parents.

Myths:

- If the adopted parents do a good job, the adoptee will not have trouble trusting others.
- The adoptive parents made up for the loss of the original family.
- The adoptee should get a good sense of self from her adoptive family.

Facts:

- Adoptees have difficulty trusting anything in a world that separated them from their natural family.
- Nothing can make up for the loss of the adoptee's natural family.
- Since the adoptee believes she was unlovable, it is very difficult for her to have a good sense of self.

Relationships are difficult for many reasons. Trust is of the greatest concern and causes great difficulty for adoptees in relationships. Adoptees have a hard time developing a close relationship with people, because if one could not trust one's own mother to stay with her, why would one trust anyone else to stay in a relationship with her? Since the natural mother and the adoptee did not get to continue their relationship, the first relationship the adoptee ever experienced, there is no solid foundation or model for the development of normal adult relationships. No matter what kind of relationship the adoptee and her

> People often say they are overwhelmed when what they really mean is that they are *afraid* they will be overwhelmed. If one is truly overwhelmed, I suspect one would be on the floor, under the table sucking one's thumb. Since the way we refer to our state of mind affects our state of mind, I have chosen to use the word whelmed as a substitute where it seems to be appropriate.

adoptive parents had, the knowledge of the failure of the natural mother/child relationship haunts the adoptee. Therefore, the closer an adoptee gets to someone, the greater the risk of her feeling shattered by any sort of rejection.

Every time an adoptee experiences any sort of loss, it is likely to touch upon the pain of losing her mother at the beginning of life. If this pain is not acknowledged or resolved, each loss will compound the pain of that original loss, so that the adoptee feels a *whelming* feeling of pain even if the trigger is relatively minor. It is common for an adoptee experiencing a break up in a relationship to feel as though she will actually die as a result of the loss. As stated earlier, this feeling relates back to the loss of her natural mother, which is why the rejection of a lover feels more devastatingly painful than one might expect.

When an adoptee enters into a romantic relationship, she often seeks individuals who represent her idealized natural mother, whether she is conscious

> **FEAR** may often be attributable to False Evidence Appearing Real.

of it or not. (There are three stereotypes which adoptees are often drawn to: the negative depiction of women who give their children up for adoption, being sleazy or loose, or a toothless alcoholic old hag, being called "the bad seed," or the idealized all-American, innocent dream girl.) Adoptees often vacillate between the two, not judging the person's true values, rather looking for an image that induces any sort of good feeling which can be as simple as not being rejected. Most often, those who follow this pattern of choosing their partners are unaware that there is any link between their behavior and the fact that they were given up at birth.

Adoptees often enter into a series of broken and unhealthy relationships. In a research study that I did on adoptees and their relationships, it was found that the average adoptee completing the survey had two marriages, and a large number of very quick, intense, spontaneous affairs. This intensity appears to be related to the longing for the natural mother relationship, and the trauma of its absence. This research also found that aside from the large percentage of people who had many tumultuous past encounters, there were 20% of adults (average age 32) who had never had any love relationships at all – no intimate relationship ever.

The apprehension related to developing intimate relationships is also linked to the adoptee's fear that someone will see a defect in her. This fear, often unconscious, is due to adoptee's firm belief, formed just before the *fracture*, that there must have been a defect which caused her to be given up at birth. Often, adoptees feel that they do not deserve to be loved because there must be something inherently wrong with them if their own mother did not want to keep them.

Due to this conclusion, adoptees often end up in relationships that are abusive to varying degrees. They feel that they do not deserve anything better, and that this may even be an appropriate punishment for the "defect" which they surely possess.

What is important for adoptees to realize is that the natural mother's decision to give them up had nothing to do with any of their inherent qualities or characteristics. All babies are lovable and deserving of affection and positive attention. To feel unlovable is perhaps to feel like one would be annihilated. Many adoptees have a hard time understanding this. One adoptee in her mid-twenties felt that when she entered therapy, she would find out about a part of herself that would destroy her – that thing that made her unlovable. This individual had panic attacks in therapy about this very issue, and dreams about aliens from outer space who would destroy her and suck her out into outer-space if she discovered that bad part of herself.

When adoptees find themselves in abusive relationships, though they are unhappy, they often prefer to remain in their situation, rather than go through the intense pain of breaking up. As discussed above, the fear of any loss is so great due to its relating back to the pain of the original loss at birth, that even a tumultuous and dangerous relationship may seem worth maintaining, if that pain can be avoided.

As is often the case in abusive relationships, the abusive partner is emotionally unavailable to the partner being abused. Adoptees are attracted to these individuals because it coincides with the adoptee's desire to find an individual who truly represents her natural mother, who is the epitome of unavailability. The unconscious behavior described here is called *repetition compulsion*. This means that an adoptee will actually find individuals who are sure to leave. The

> Repetition compulsion is an unconscious attempt to resolve childhood conflicts through adult relationships that mimic the behaviors and conflicts of the past. They are therefore doomed to fail.

adoptee is repeatedly attracted to partners who will treat her in an abusive or emotionally unavailable manner, and the adoptee will compulsively attempt to get this person to change his ways and treat the adoptee in a more lovable and affectionate manner. The hope to have her partner change his behavior reflects the adoptee's wish that her natural mother will change her own behavior and come back and provide love and never leave the adoptee again. However, since the natural mother never changed her ways by coming back and being available, the adult adoptee will never be satisfied unless her partner sticks to his abusive behavior as well. Therefore, the situation is a catch-22 because if the dream of having the partner change his behavior is realized, the adoptee will not be satisfied because then the relationship does not really mirror the mother equals loss pattern.

If an adoptee accidentally picks someone who will not leave, someone who is somehow available to the adoptee whether they are abusive or not, then the adoptee will very often feel unconsciously compelled to sabotage the relationship. It is truly intolerable to think that anyone can truly be there for her. The message that stays in the head of the adoptee is that being truly loved is a disaster, because the partner will definitely leave, recreating the intolerable loss of her mother at the beginning of her life. It feels like a tremendous risk to remain at this point in a relationship.

In order to develop a successful adult relationship, it is crucial that the adoptee understand that the intense fear of having a lover leave her is because the lover represents her natural mother. Then the adoptee can learn how to watch her demands of neediness in a relationship, or can be with someone who feels free to say, "Well it seems like you're asking me to mommy you right now." If an adoptee is open to hearing that because she has done enough personal work, she has reached a very healthy stage in relationship development. She can then have good relationships; but she just has to do more work than other people.

Adoptees often focus more on their own needs in a relationship, relating back to their original needs which were not met in their first relationship ever – with their natural mothers. No matter how often they try to have them filled, these needs will never be fully met in adult relationships, because it is impossible to have as an adult what you should have had as a baby and thereby replace the void. Additionally, adoptees are often too needy, expecting the partner to always be there, constantly assisting with any small task. It is not always said, but it's inherent in the relationship that the adoptee wants to be taken care of, and this often creates a suffocating atmosphere for her partner, which may scare her partner off. When the adoptee fears an ultimate breakup, she often becomes more needy and clingy, due to the fear of experiencing the pain of yet another loss which is reminiscent of losing her natural mother.

Another obstacle which adoptees often face when searching for an adult relationship is the lack of any hopes for the future. Without a sense of past, it is very difficult to dream of the future, or have any concept of wants, desires or relationships related to what is yet to happen. Without knowledge of how you started your life, it can be very difficult to know how to continue. One adoptee related that she felt like she was never going to reach the age of 21, and never felt like there was a future for her. Many other adoptees never thought they would reach the age of thirty – they just felt like it was not going to happen, because their past was unknown.

As discussed in earlier chapters, the third trauma – the fracture – caused the adoptee to cut off all feelings because they were too painfully connected to the original loss of the natural mother. This also creates a sense of not being aware of one's wants and desires, because there are no gut feelings to guide the adoptee. They are hidden "under ice." In choosing romantic partners, adoptees often are not aware of warning bells which would normally serve to warn an individual from entering into an unhealthy relationship. Interestingly, a common thread in many adoptee relationships is that they have a tendency to let people choose them.

This also connects back to the way their second relationship evolved. Adoptees were chosen by their adoptive parents, who ultimately were the ones who expressed whatever love, affection and security they were exposed to. This was the second model for developing relationships that the adoptee "witnessed", and often impacts the method of entering into adult relationships. If an adoptee meets someone who chooses to have a relationship with her, then there is a feeling of being stuck and not having a choice to get out of the relationship, because that was the way she was found by her adoptive parents in the first place. The adoptee "chooses" to let the other person love her. Then, if the adoptee would like to leave her partner, this seems impossible, because that would touch upon unconscious feelings of wanting to leave the adoptive parents, which would be a betrayal and is associated with painful feelings which the adoptee does not like to acknowledge.

In order to avoid this and many other conflicts, one thing that can be done is for the adoptive parents to find a way to discuss pain and loss issues openly with the adoptee. Another thing to do is to open up adoptions, so that adoptees can meet their natural mothers, and see them, and therefore know that they are real people. Hopefully, the adoptee would hear a reasonable story about why her natural mother is not with her, and hear from her natural mother that she is loved by her.

Adoptees often have conflicted relationships with their adoptive parents. From the adoptee's point of view, their adoptive parents are to "blame" for everything. If their parents had given birth to them as they were supposed to, they wouldn't have lost a family, wouldn't be adopted, and wouldn't have all this pain. Also, if their parents hadn't adopted them, why they would still be with their natural parents. Again, no loss, no pain. In addition, adoptees and their adoptive parents are very often on different wave lengths, different ways of being in the world which may be genetically predisposed and which can make communication more difficult.

Finally, the ghost of the birth family resides in the adoptive home, so there are unspoken thoughts and feelings that need to be dealt with or there is extra tension in the family.

If the adoptive parents could only share their own pain, it would likely free up the adoptee to share her pain and lead to a closer understanding and better relationship between family members. A mutual sharing can lead to a mutual closeness.

It is important to note, that without a reunion, the adoptee's ability to accept her adoptive parents as "real" is more difficult and the idealization of her natural parents may continue to interfere, not only with her romantic relationships, but with her relationship with her adoptive parents as well.

To Summarize

- Adoptees very often have difficulty with close relationships.
- Adoptees very often have difficulty finding a career that suits them.
- Adoptees are very often afraid to face their own truth.
- All these difficulties are surmountable with work.

Exercise

- Close your eyes and try to picture yourself at age seven. Walk into the picture and stand in front of that young person that you were. Out loud in your head, say, "Hi, I've come back to visit you again." Remind your inner child that you have been taking care of her all these years and though she may be scared, you've been protecting her quite well indeed. Tell her that it is okay to get close to people and ask her how she feels about that statement. Ask her what she is feeling after hearing you say that. Tell her it is okay to feel whatever she says she is feeling. Remind her that what happened in the beginning can never happen again. Tell her that the more she lets herself feel her true feelings and tells them to you, the adult, the easier it will be to pick people with whom it is safe to enter into a relationship.

Experience of the Moment

*   You might be experiencing some anxiety as a result of your conversation with your inner child. You might be feeling a bit hopeless and vulnerable. These feelings are not pleasant at all, but they are to be expected and they will not hurt you, just make you uncomfortable. It is truly all right and healthy to experience your feelings, no matter what they are. You need to build up your tolerance for uncomfortable feelings to be able to do your healing. Why not visualize giving your inner child a hug. Say, "I love you" to her and tell her to relax, she is safe. Say, "I know it doesn't feel like it but we're okay."

Chapter 8:

Limbo: The Purgatory
of Not Knowing the Truth

As was stated earlier, the future is blind without sight of the past. The effect on the lives of adopted people who do not know the truth of their origins is a prime example of this adage. If the adoptee does not know the truth about why she was given up, then she may never (unless she does a lot of work similar to that outlined in this book) really trust anyone to stay in a relationship with her. Her relationships may abound with difficulties as a result.

The relationship difficulties encountered in early adulthood increase as adoptees approach, consider or enter into marriage and parenthood. A number of factors place adoptee marriages at risk, including a general distrust of others, the tendency to pick rejecting people as mates, jealousy and/or fear of abandonment, and the tendency on the part of both sexes to choose idealized mothers as mates.

Having children is often unsettling for adoptees. The birth of a child obviously reminds adoptees of their own birth and natural parents. When his wife becomes a mother, a male adoptee may want her to be his mother and/or may identify her with the mother who abandoned him. A female adoptee, on the other hand, identifies with both her own natural mother and her infant, and often becomes overprotective of her child. There is also the strong possibility of unconscious jealousy and rage at her child. After all, her child is getting what she didn't get: The opportunity to grow up with her birth family. This is something to be aware of for all adoptees who choose to parent.

Adoptees of both sexes continue to have difficulty focusing on what to do with their lives. This, and the tendency to feel infantalized and to act childlike in work as well as in personal relationships, contributes to continued difficulties in establishing themselves in a career.

Certain events in adoptees' adult lives – such as marriage, pregnancy/birth of a child, or the death of an adoptive parent – often trigger a surfacing of repressed emotional conflict surrounding their own birth and surrender. It is at this time that many adoptees begin to search and perhaps to seek therapy, although they may be unwilling or unable at this point to acknowledge that adoption is an issue for them.

Myths:

- If an adoptee looks happy and well adjusted, she is.
- If an adoptee decides to seek the truth, she is emotionally unbalanced.
- If an adoptee searches, she is looking to get even or get rich.

Facts:

- Many people who appear happy are just (unconsciously) hiding pain.

- It is normal and healthy for an adoptee to want to know her own truth, her own beginnings.
- Adoptees search to complete their identity.

As Betty Jean Lifton[6] states, most adoptees have a searcher and non-searcher inside them. If the non-searcher is dominant, the adoptee can avoid feeling the pain of losing her natural family, feelings of abandonment and lack of self-worth. Some adoptees never search, because the fears appear to be too much to handle. The pain, sadness and anger are brewing and the adoptee must keep these feelings under ice because it feels like the feelings will kill her. Her very survival depends on the success of her defense mechanisms of denial and/or repression.

Whatever feelings a person keeps under the surface still affect her life and her relationships. Intimate relationships very often don't feel safe for adoptees. After all, the person who should have been the most trustworthy to have a relationship with "abandoned" her. (That's not what happened, but it is what it feels like to the adoptee.)

Not knowing the truth about one's life places one in *limbo*, between reality and fantasy. The adoptee is stuck in between and isn't even consciously aware of the situation or the pain of it. Aside from the internal pain, being in *limbo* affects the adoptee's life in a myriad of ways.

Relationships are commonly very troublesome for adoptees and the relationship difficulties that adoptees have present themselves in a variety of ways:

The adoptee often lives emotionally in what Betty Jean Lifton

---

[6] Betty Jean Lifton, *Journey of the Adopted Self*

and Bob Andersen[7] refer to as the "Ghost Kingdom," the world that she feels she would have lived in had she not been adopted, having secret loving relationships with those that fit her fantasy of her idealized natural mother. It matters not what the sex of the adoptee or her partner is.   As soon as one has a strong connection to another as a potential partner, the relationship may well enter the realm of natural mother "Fantasyland."   The Ghost Kingdom is a much safer place to have a relationship than the real world, after all.

The adoptee picks rejecting people, (repetition compulsion) attempting to resolve the loss of her natural mother. (This time her partner, who is the representation of her mother, no matter what sex her partner is, will realize her mistake and not reject her.) Unfortunately, for her partner to be a representation of her natural mother, her partner must be a rejector or somehow unavailable.

> "I don't believe we didn't want our mother's love...I believe we desperately want it from the beginning and never stop, but every day, every minute, every second that goes by, makes it more and more painful to accept the love. It hurts too damn much to get what you always wanted and 'see' it. To truly understand what we have lost seems like it will kill us and so we reject it, out of hand."
> Male adoptee, age 48

The adoptee pushes others to leave her, knowing it will happen eventually, or believing that she deserves it to happen. She will stay in a bad or abusive relationship, because she cannot tolerate endings or she believes she deserves the bad relationship.

The adoptee is often very jealous of her partner's outside relationships, fearing abandonment just the way her natural mother abandoned her. If her natural mother abandoned her, why wouldn't everyone else abandon her.   The closer or more intimate the relationship, the greater the risk to the adoptee if the relationship ends. The adoptee often cannot tolerate this risk at all and will do

---

[7] Robert Andersen & Rhonda Tucker. *The Bridge Less Traveled*

anything to stop the intimacy.

Adoptees of both sexes often pick idealized mothers as mates, even if their mate is male. It seems that any love interest at this stage of the adoptee's life will be a representation of mommy in the purest sense. These relationships are very emotionally dangerous because the adoptee can be re-abandoned by mommy at any moment. The mate can never live up to the adoptee's expectations unless they leave, which is what the adoptee expects.

Adoptees often feel and act infantalized in relationships – job as well as marriage. The adoptee is unconsciously used to being treated as a child and creates situations where she is treated that way. Even the law in most states never allows for the adopted person to be referred to as anything but a child.

As was stated earlier, adoptees can have many difficulties parenting their own children: Having children is often unsettling because it reminds the adoptee of her own beginnings and the lack of information about her own creation.

For a male adoptee: when his wife becomes a mother, he wants her as his own mother, and is often jealous of the time spent with the newborn. His wife becomes the mother who abandoned him and she is giving what he didn't get to her baby (mothering from his natural mother).

For a female adoptee: she identifies with both her own mother and her infant. A female adoptee is often jealous of her own baby, because she is giving her baby what she herself didn't get (mothering from her natural mother). She is often overprotective, unsure of herself as a mother because of the mothering she did and didn't get. Adopted females often want to adopt a child, somehow believing they are giving back from being "rescued".

At this stage of the adoptee's life, there is often a general uneasiness about herself and the world. She can't trust the world or others. Why should she? The world started off unsafe and nobody fixed it. If she couldn't trust her own mother to keep her, why should she trust anyone else. Additionally, because adoptees so often pick the wrong partner, being "rejected" just proves or reinforces that the world is unsafe and no one is to be trusted.

The adoptee is continually having difficulty focusing on what she is going to do with her life. If her basic feelings are hidden from her, then how can she possibly know what she wants to do with her life? The adoptee needs to get in touch with all of her feelings to be able to know what she wants to do.

Lastly, there is the continuing attempt of the adoptee to fight acknowledgment of her adoption issues, yet there are constant triggers in life to the adoptee's beginnings: marriage, pregnancy and birth; death of a parent, baby food commercials, a baby in a stroller, the loss of a relationship, etc. All of these trigger the original "abandonment" as the adoptee approaches her fear of her feelings. She is running around like a clown with all those sticks in the air, plates a-spinning on top, trying to keep everything in order, trying not to feel the terror of her beginnings.

In general, as human beings, we need to recognize that we need to (when we are ready) walk into our pain and our fear. They are both signposts to our healing path. We need to respect our fear. Think about the fear you feel now and remember that you felt this same fear as a child and had to deal with it alone. You survived that then **without** support, so you should be able to survive it now **with** support.

Please don't ever forget this!

All of the above difficulties are changeable. Adoptees can

learn to pick well and have good relationships, be good parents and find their way in the world. It is unfair that it takes work and a commitment, but the rewards are phenomenal and the alternative, well... you know what that is like.

To Summarize

- Adoptees often have a great deal of difficulty finding a partner.
- Adoptees often have a great deal of difficulty finding a career that fits.
- Adoptees spend a lot of time in denial of their beginnings.
- All of the difficulties can be addressed and therefore be less troublesome.

Exercise

- Close your eyes and try to imagine what it would be like if you could talk to your natural mother. What would you want to ask her? What might you want her to say and do? What are your feelings about her? Are you glad she gave you up? If not, what *do* you feel about what happened to you? What are your feelings toward her? Anger? Love? Resentment? Are your feelings all bundled up, interwoven?

  You might want to write your different feelings about your mother and what happened to you in your journal. You might want to do this often and notice that the feelings change over time. Anger one day... Sadness the next ... tenderness the next, then back to anger etc. All of this is normal. Your feelings about what happened are among the most confusing feelings possible. Keeping track and trying to separate your feelings will ultimately help you in many ways in your life.

Experience of the Moment

- You might be experiencing some confusion right now. Or even deep fear. If so, take a deep breath and say the word RELAX out loud in your head. No matter what you are feeling right now, try to write it down and try to connect what you are feeling now with the exercise above and perhaps with the chapter you have just finished. It would be understandable that what you have just read has stirred you up. It would also be understandable for you not to be able to make a connection between what you read and your feelings. Our feelings do not come from nowhere. Neither do adoptees! Please know that your feelings won't kill you. They are just feelings. Scary, yes. Painful, yes. However, they won't kill... even though it feels that way. If you are still feeling shaky, look around you and verify that nothing is happening and then say out loud in your head, "Nothing is happening now. I know it feels like it, but we're okay." Repeat this a few times until you feel better. Then recognize that you are indeed okay.

Part Two:

The Search for Self

The problems, issues, and techniques involved in providing effective healing for adoptees

The vast majority of psychotherapists lack the skills to address the specific problems of adoptees. Since adoptees are likely to say that adoption is not an issue for them, or often do not even mention that they are adopted, it is easy for therapists to miss adoption-related dynamics. More importantly, an adoptee's life experience directly challenges much of what therapists have been taught professionally and it also attacks other deeply entrenched, often unconsciously held assumptions. Because an adoptee's existential experience is completely different from that of a non-adoptee, therapists (unless they are adopted) have little in their own experience to draw on as a means of relating to clients who were adopted. Finally, if the therapist is an adoptive parent, she may have an unconscious vested interest in not acknowledging the destructive impact of surrender/adoption on the psychosocial development of a child.

> "When you turn the corner,/ And you run into yourself,/ Then you know that you have turned,/ all the corners that are left" – *The Final Curve* – Langston Hughes

Part Two discusses the problems, issues, and techniques

involved in providing effective psychotherapy for adoptees. Particular emphasis is placed on what is different about treating adoptees, the traps therapist are likely to fall into, and special techniques that are helpful in working with adoptees.

Although much of this section focuses on the professional treatment of adoptees, there is a great deal of information that will be useful to natural mothers, adoptive parents, and adoptees themselves. Since the problems of most adoptees are not obvious enough to motivate their parents to seek treatment for them as infants or children, adoptees do not usually enter therapy until adolescence or adulthood.

Thus, most adoptees' "therapists" during childhood are their adoptive parents. There are many things that loving and informed adoptive parents can do to help heal the wounds of separation and avoid the fracturing of their child's sense of self. Conversely, any unresolved issues they might have around adoption are guaranteed to adversely affect the child's development. Chapter Nine deals with the necessity for pregnant women and adoptive parents to confront these issues *before* surrender/adoption – not only for their child's sake, but for their own.

Chapters 10-13 are addressed as much to adoptive parents as to therapists. These chapters contain practical suggestions that adoptive parents can use to recognize and deal with their child's difficulties during infancy and childhood.

As adolescents are capable of taking an active role in their healing process, Chapter 14 is addressed to both teenage adoptees and their adoptive parents.

Finally, Chapter 15 presents ways in which adult adoptees can begin to take control over their adoption experience and "repair" the psychological damage they may have sustained.

Special attention is given to dealing with the emotional upheaval involved in searching and reuniting with natural mothers. Parts of Chapter 15 are directed to those providing counseling and psychotherapy to adolescent and adult adoptees. However, much of this information will be of use to adoptees and their spouses, adoptive parents and natural parents, as well.

Chapter 9:

The Truth Hurts

Natural parents and adoptive parents typically experience enormous emotional pain at the time adoption takes place. Rather than being helped by those around them to deal with their emotional conflicts, both sets of parents are usually led to believe that the pain will go away once adoption has been finalized. Adoption becomes a permanent solution to a temporary problem.

We need to look at the realities of adoption for natural parents and adoptive parents, stressing the need for all of them to receive help in dealing with the emotional trauma that has brought them to this point. It is clearly best if parents confront these issues *before* surrendering/adopting a child, but if that cannot be done, these issues will have to be addressed as soon as possible if the natural mother and adoptive parents are to be able to fully relate to the adoptee.

Adoptive parents must understand that adoption is not a cure for infertility nor a way of erasing the sorrow and loss of self-esteem inherent in not being able to reproduce. For the adoptive family to function well, the prospective parents must fully understand and mourn their loss of fertility and they must also recognize that raising an adopted child is not the same as raising a birth child and that an adoptive family is not the same as a birth family.

Although an adoptive family will not and cannot be like a birth family, it does **not** mean that the family can't function well or be a loving family. For this to happen, however, adoptive parents must be prepared to accept the adoptive family for what it is, not as a facsimile for what they were unable to have.

At the same time, the frightened pregnant mother must know that surrendering her child will have a life-long effect on her and her baby. She must understand what some of these effects may be in order to make an informed decision about surrender and, if she chooses that option, to deal constructively with adoption-related issues that may come up for her later in life.

Myths:

- Adopting a baby will remove the pain of infertility.
- Adoptive families are just like any other family and adoptive parenting is just the same.
- Women who lose babies to adoption soon forget and go on with their lives.
- An adopted child doesn't experience the loss of the natural family.

Facts:

- Adoption does not remove the pain of infertility.
- Adoptive families are indeed different and adoptive parenting is also different.
- Women who lose babies to adoption *never* forget and their loss is unresolvable.

- Babies *do* experience the loss of their mothers, even when the separation begins at birth.

Hopefully, both pregnant women and adoptive parents will deal with these issues before surrender/adoption. If they do not, the problems must be addressed eventually, for the sake of the adoptee and all of the parents.

The inability to bring a child into a family by birth, is very painful indeed. The loss of this ability may cause the couple to believe that they are a failure. The parent who is unable to procreate may feel incomplete. These are deep, narcissistic wounds and need to be addressed.

The loss of fertility needs to be mourned, the genetic child that would have been needs to be mourned, and the relationship with that child needs to be mourned as well.

If these wounds are left untreated, and grieving is not attended to, one's ability to parent an adopted child may be severely hampered. The adopted child will be a constant reminder of the child that could have been and there may well be unconscious resentment of the child for not being a birth child.

> "My belief (as an adoptee) is that our mothers are not the objects of our discomfort. What *is* the object of our discomfort is the respect we never got and the grieving and pain of losing our mothers. Our discomfort is in facing the reality of our losses, the truths we didn't have growing up, believing we were unlovable because we weren't kept. Even if the terrible separation occurs, if we are given the respect of truth, of a reunion around age 7 or 8, of photos and stories and the gift of being able to feel our own feelings, we would not push our mothers away."
> Female adoptee, age 57

Moreover, the child may unconsciously be seen as a failure

for not being able to take away the parents' pain, for not looking like them, not acting like them and not being like them. It is extremely important to recognize these issues and attend to them. Left alone or ignored, the family dynamics will likely deteriorate, emotional upheaval will spread and the relationships will then suffer.

There is no substitute for good grief counseling for the adoptive parents. We wouldn't dream of telling someone whose parent dies not to grieve their loss. The loss of the child that could have been is no less painful than the death of a parent. Different yes, but just as painful and the respect of mourning one's losses is paramount. Moreover, if the adoptive parents cannot deal with the pain of their losses, how can they possibly deal with the pain of their adopted child's loss of her natural family.

The pregnant mother needs to understand that surrendering her child to adoption is only one of several options. The decision to place a baby for adoption is in most cases irrevocable. In most states, open adoption, while a more humane choice for all involved, is not legally binding and is often used as a "sales-tool" by the adoption agency or lawyer.

The experience of losing a child to adoption is no different than the experience of losing a child to death, except, there are no photos, no knowing if the child is alive, happy, healthy etc. The child vanishes forever, much like someone who has gone off to war and is "missing in action." The child will be missing in adoption. The fact is that in a similar fashion, the child experiences the death of her mother when placed for adoption.

You may encounter many adopted people along the way who will tell you that being relinquished for adoption hasn't affected them at all. The adopted individuals might even say they are glad they were given up. This is most likely denial of the highest order. You may also encounter natural mothers who might say they weren't affected by giving up their child. This too, is most likely denial of the highest order. It would seem unlikely that the real loss of a mother or baby would *not* leave its mark on those involved and every effort must be made to keep the baby within the mother's family.

Our society looks at adoption as a panacea ... " Win-Win." In fact, every adoption begins with huge losses for all involved. The natural mother loses her baby, the baby loses her mother and the adoptive parents have lost their genetic child.   All those contemplating adoption need to pay attention to these losses in advance and not pretend that all who are involved will be happy.

If the mother truly cannot keep her baby within her family, and if all those involved deal with the realities of adoption, the mothers may have the opportunity to receive support and comfort to help them deal with their losses in a healthy way and be in an open adoption. Burying our heads in the sand means we will get kicked in the behind and not see it coming.

To Summarize

- All those involved in adoption have suffered large losses.
- It is much healthier to deal with truth.
- Adoptive parents need to grieve their losses before they adopt.
- Pregnant women need to know the truth about the consequences of surrendering a child to adoption both for themselves and their child before they surrender.

Exercise

- If you are an adoptive parent, write down all your feelings about not being able to bring a child into your family other than through adoption.

- If you are a pregnant woman, write down all the feelings you have for the unborn child you are carrying.

- If you are not one of the above, try to put yourself in their shoes and write down what you might feel if you were in their situation.

Experience of the Moment

- You might be feeling confused, scared or sad or all of these emotions. Anyone would likely feel that way. All humans need to be able to feel sad about sad things. As humans, we need to be able to grieve our losses and cry about them, as that is the only way to mourn. It is truly painful to cry, but crying lets the pain out. Keeping the pain and sadness inside is destructive. Letting it out is truly healing.

Chapter 10:

Triage: Treating
the Primal Wound

The newborn infant who has been surrendered to adoption
has just experienced the loss of all of her favorite things. (Now is
probably a good time to read Appendix E: *Loss in the Adoption
Hand-off*. The baby has lost her mother's voice, body sounds and
rhythms, smell and touch. She has lost the opportunity to gaze into
her eyes and to lie against *her* skin.

The newborn child has lost the most precious and sacred
relationship in the world and she knows it. As a result, she may
react by pushing her new mom away, she may be restless in her
arms, and she may stiffen up when held. This is not unusual
behavior and probably has nothing to do with the new mother doing
something wrong. It is likely due to the baby being in unfamiliar
surroundings.

The new parents need to recognize that the newborn has just
suffered one of the worst losses in the world and needs to grieve.
It is not a time of happiness for the new baby, rather a time of
enormous sadness.

Myths:

- Babies don't know one mother from another.
- Babies don't suffer the loss of their natural mother.
- Babies are babies and all can be treated alike.

Facts:

- Babies are aware of the loss of their natural mothers.
- Babies suffer from the loss of their mothers.
- Babies need special attention and consideration when they have lost their mothers.

As an adoptive mother, you won't "smell right" to your new born. You won't sound right or even look right, but you mustn't take your child's reaction personally. It is important not to respond to rejection with rejection or withdrawal. Build up slowly to hugs; let the baby become accustomed to your smell, movements, etc. Talk slowly and softly to your baby remembering that she is hurting badly and needs to feel safe and secure. She needs soft soothing sounds, motions and touch. Give her time. If she pushes away, she is only reacting to the loss of her natural mother.

Your baby may cry a lot. If so, comfort her as much as she needs to feel safe. Your baby may be relatively quiet. No matter what *face* your baby presents to you, bear in mind that she has just had a severe loss. Adults who suffer a loss may react in many different ways on the surface, but that does not change the underlying sadness

> "The child...shall, wherever possible, grow up in the care and under the responsibility of his parents... a child of tender years shall not, save in exceptional circumstances, be separated from his mother." – *Declaration of the Rights of the Child,* – United Nations/UNICEF

that accompanies loss.

You should assume your baby is distressed and give TLC whether or not it is obviously needed. Your baby knows that something is wrong, but she doesn't have any way to express it verbally. Your baby experienced the loss of her favorite things and it may take some time for her to feel secure. Be patient with her, always understanding, always calm and always soothing.

To Summarize

- Your baby lost her favorite things in the world when she lost her natural mother.

- Your baby needs all the TLC that you can give her.

- Your baby may need a good amount of time and reassurance and soothing talk before she will be as responsive to you as you would like.

- Your baby is hurting and cannot explain it to you. You need to understand this and make allowances for her pain.

Exercise

- Try to imagine what it would feel like if you experienced a natural disaster such as a tornado or hurricane and you survived, but all your family were killed and all your possessions were destroyed, except for the clothes on your back. What would that be like? How would you cope? What would you do? Your baby just survived a disaster or trauma of the highest order and only has her new mother. Everything else that she valued or knew is gone. Write down your answers to the above exercise and keep the baby in mind as you write.

Experience of the Moment

- You might be very anxious right now, or angry or perhaps

highly discouraged. Please understand that this book is intended to educate not discourage. The purpose of this writing is to help all involved in an adoption better understand what happens to the infant. It is the infant who is supposed to be the star of this event. It is all supposed to happen for her "best interest." Yes, there will be much pain, but if you pay attention to what is written in these pages, the infant will be better taken care of, her needs more fully met; and ultimately she will be happier. The infant is what matters here. Adoption is not a panacea for anyone involved and certainly does not cure infertility or the loss of one's mother or child. That doesn't mean that in those cases where there is no other choice that the baby cannot fare well. However for the infant to fare as well as possible, the adults first have to be educated.

Chapter 11:

Really Talking About Adoption

Although telling the child that she is adopted confirms what is already known, the way in which parents convey this information will greatly influence the child's response to the conscious knowledge of adoption.

The importance of truth, honesty, and openness in talking to the child is of utmost importance. Contrary to advice commonly given to adoptive parents, they should avoid telling the child that she is special or chosen, as these are basically lies that will come back to haunt everyone concerned. Parents should also not assume that, by telling the child that she is adopted, they have dealt with the adoption issue and can "put it to rest." Telling, or the willingness to discuss adoption, should be an ongoing process throughout the child's development.

Signs of sadness, aggression or hostility are things that parents should be on the alert for and the child will need help to deal with these feelings.

Myths:

- If you tell a child that she is special or chosen she will feel good about herself.
- You shouldn't tell a child she is adopted.
- If you tell your child that her parents died in a car crash she won't think about them.

Facts:

- Telling a child she is special or chosen or lucky will not ring true and will make the child feel worse.
- Adopted children will always figure out or find out that they are adopted.
- Telling a child that her parents are dead will not stop her from thinking about them and causes a tremendous amount of extra pain and guilt for the child.

The importance of truth, honesty, and openness is paramount. Telling the child she is adopted confirms what she already knows since she was there when she lost her natural mother. A child should be allowed to experience everything she feels. The child may very well cry about her loss, be sad about the loss of her other mother and she may even say, "I miss my other Mommy." She should feel free to express all of her pain, anger and sadness about what happened to her.

> "Guilt is a hand across the eyes, a knife at the heart. There can be no peace, no joy, no ecstasy, no pride in accomplishment. With guilt, all there can be is a pseudo-life where one goes through the motions expected of an adult, and carries in her mind the horrors imagined by a child." – John D. MacDonald

Adopted children do not want to hear that they are special, chosen or lucky. Is it only special or chosen children who lose their natural mothers? As Betty Jean Lifton writes in *Lost and Found*, "If I am so special, why was I available to be chosen?" And if I am lucky, does that mean I am lucky I am not with my natural mother? What does that say about her or about me? This is confusing and painful for a child. Any adult would have trouble with the logic of this and yet, we expect being special or chosen to "make it okay" for the adopted child. Moreover, every time you say special or chosen to the child, you are pointing out she is adopted. It is like a slap in the face to keep saying you are adopted, and therefore special. Also, in terms of chosen, many adoptees believe (have a mental picture in their head) they were picked out in a sort of baby supermarket from among hundreds of babies. Not a very pleasant thought at all.

Nothing in the world, no story, *nothing* can make the loss of a child's mother okay. The best we can do is explain that it wasn't the child's fault, it wasn't because of her it happened and she is totally loveable. Then encourage her to talk about what she feels and ask questions.

There are those who suggest that the child should not be told she is adopted. This cannot be considered. First of all, the child was there and knows she lost her natural mother, even if she doesn't have words. Second, the child **will** find out, from a friend or neighbor or relative. She'll hear something, somewhere. Third, secrets are poison in families. When there is a secret, everyone knows it exists, even if they don't know the exact nature of it. Secrets cause tension for all those involved. Fourth, children always know when the adults around them are lying. Finally, when the adoptee finds out, there will be rage at having been lied to, having one's own truth withheld. She will feel betrayed by her adoptive parents.

It is important to recognize that children react to what happens to them as if it was caused by them. The adopted child will undoubtedly believe that she was given up because she was defective and the defect is her unlovability. This is very painful for a child to deal with and if not addressed, can cause great difficulty later in life. (See Chapter 13, Preventing the Fracture)

A child's drawings, play, etc. should be observed for signs of sadness, aggression or hostility. Parents should not assume that they can tell their child that she is adopted and that she will be okay, especially if the child never mentions it again. There will be anger and if it is not vocalized, it may show up in the child's play with others.

Anger not expressed in a healthy manner will surely show up another way. If anger is not talked out, then it will be acted out (against others) or acted in (against oneself) in terms of substance abuse, physical ailments or in some other negative form of expression.

We need to tell the child the truth in an age-appropriate fashion, in ways that can be understood and dealt with by someone her age. Children need answers that are true and make sense, otherwise, the world feels unsafe for them.

What should adoptive parents do or say to help their child in this stage of her healing? First, if possible, they should begin to deal with their own pain of infertility (if infertility is a factor). The parents need to be comfortable talking about adoption, or their child (of any age) will find it difficult to address the subject. They should acknowledge the child's sadness, pain and anger at her losses.

They should tell their child that it's okay to feel and think whatever she is feeling and thinking. Hopefully the adoptive parents can acknowledge their own sadness about their child's losses. They should let their child cry and hold her if possible. Understand that she may push them away because she wants comfort from her other mother. Trying to comfort her may make her angry. Acknowledge this if it happens. Providing the child with a reunion and the truth about her life before she experiences the fracture can stop the fracture, or at least minimize it and help her.

Try to avoid saying you know what it feels like. The adoptee knows that anyone who hasn't walked in her shoes cannot possibly know what it feels like. Show caring and empathy. We need to bear in mind that the adopted child may not be aware of having any feelings at all (about adoption or otherwise), or she may just not have the words to express her emotions. It can take a lot of time for the adoptee to feel safe experiencing these most terrorizing of feelings, a fear of annihilation and a fear of the destructive potential of her rage. She is unlikely to be consciously aware of such feelings.

The adoptive parents can say, "That must be painful or sad for you," etc. as an acknowledgment. Validate! Validate! Validate! For the adopted child (and later the adult) the big questions are: Who, What, Where, When, How and Why. Simply put, these translate to: Did she love me? Does she love me? Who is she? Why did she give me up? Did she think about me all these years? Where is she? What do I want to tell her? What do I want to hear? Will she want to see me? Children deserve and need to feel safe. Having real answers to real questions helps them feel safe.

The "Car Crash" story was told to thousands of adoptees. The expected result is the belief on the part of the adoptee that she killed her parents in some way. She feels guilt for surviving, and she might picture a car wreck with dead parents within. This not a pleasant aftermath. If lies in general are poison to relationships, this one is close to deadly and must never even be considered. There is no reason to try to make believe that an adopted child's natural parents are dead. This will only cause more unbearable pain for the child who has already suffered a terrible loss.

We have discussed "as if" earlier in this book. Just to review: To tell a child that she is loved "as if" she was a child born to the family, causes pain. The child knows it *cannot* be true. You may love a child greatly, perhaps even more than a biological child, but "as if" cannot work. I cannot love my cat as if she is a dog and parents cannot love an adopted child the same or "as if" she was born to the family. It is impossible to do because it is not so. Also, every time you tell the child she is loved "as if" you are telling her she is not the same as everyone else. Just saying, "I love you" says it all and does not need to be qualified.

To Summarize

- Adopted children need to hear the truth about their beginnings.

- Secrecy and lies are poisonous and cause dysfunctional families.

- Adopted children will believe they are to blame for being given up and we need to help them understand the fallacy of that belief.

Exercise

- Write down your thoughts and feelings about what you have just read. What troubles you? What don't you understand? Do you disagree with what you have read, or simply not like it? If you need to, go back and read again. We must not forget that adoption is about the best interest of the child, not the adults. We must always put the child's feelings and best interest first.

Experience of the Moment

- You might be experiencing some anger and anxiety about what you just read. It is normal to be anxious and angry about what is written here. None of these realities of adoption are fun or pleasant, but they are necessary to understand if we truly have the child's best interest at heart.

Chapter 12:

Ghost Busters

The ghost of the natural parents lives in every adoptive home. It is important for all family members to acknowledge the reality of the natural parents of the adoptee. To deny their existence, denies the existence of the adoptee and denies the feelings that all family members have about the natural parents.

Myths:

- The adoptee never thinks about her natural parents.

- There is no need to acknowledge that the natural parents ever existed.

Facts:

- The adoptee is thinking about her natural parents often, even if unconsciously.

- The adoptive parents are also thinking about the natural parents often, even if unconsciously.

- Everyone in the family must openly acknowledge the existence of the natural parents.

Children need to understand the way the world around them works to feel safe. The adoptee is constantly struggling with the questions of *who, what, where, when, how* and *why* in trying to understand her world and the answers that are not normally forthcoming. In order to feel safe, the adoptee needs answers. All these questions refer to the facts of the adoptee's existence. The lack of answers leads to the formation, in the adoptee's head, of the ghosts of her natural parents. When her natural parents are not acknowledged, their ghosts "haunt" the house and everyone is frightened by their feelings about what the ghosts represent.

The way to remove the ghosts is to bring the reality of the birth family into the adoptive home. The adoptive parents can, when the opportunity arises, say, "Your mother must have been a wonderful artist or a good athlete," depending on the talents or aptitudes displayed by the adopted child.

The child must be encouraged to talk about her birth family, particularly her natural mother with whom she had that most important connection. Talking about the birth family will relieve tension in the house, allowing everyone to act more naturally. If the adoptive parents have photographs of birth family members (which they should certainly try to obtain) sharing them with their child will be most helpful.

> "Adoptees, then, are caught between the loyalty they feel to the adoptive parents who 'rescued' them and the invisible loyalty to the mother who gave birth to them. Troubled as they are by feeling ungrateful, they remain ambivalent about accepting their adoptive parents as the 'real' ones. Yet because they have not had real experiences in the real world with the natural mother, they cannot accept her as real either. Their split loyalties prevent them from resolving their issues with either set of parents."
> *Journey of the Adopted Self*
> – Betty Jean Lifton

Children will, as they grow up, look at their parents as good one moment (when they do what the child wants) and bad the next minute (when mommy and daddy don't). One of the child's developmental tasks is to eventually (hopefully) understand that mommy and daddy are neither all good nor all bad.

The adopted child has a much more formidable problem to solve. Aside from splitting her adoptive parents into good or bad, she has the reality of the natural parents being bad for giving her up, but good if they might come rescue her. Then her adoptive parents at the same time become good if she thinks they will not be angry at her being rescued or bad if they will be angry. This internal conflict is terrifying and very difficult to sort out. Thinking of either parent as bad causes the terror of being abandoned just for thinking such "terrible or bad" thoughts. Her adoptive mom may be good one day when she thinks of her birthmom as bad and vice-versa. This kind of flip-flop splitting is normal and should not be a cause for alarm.

The adoptive parents need to reinforce their love for their child, reminding their child when necessary that some behaviors are not acceptable, and immediately affirming their love. When their child gets angry at them, they need to acknowledge it by saying something like, "I'm sorry you are angry about _____ . I love you." "Honey would you draw mommy a picture of your anger?" The parents then need to compliment the picture of the child's anger.

Anger will be a common emotion in an adopted child and why not? Doesn't she have a lot to be angry about? The most important thing to do is to validate the child's anger, understand the splitting and find ways for the child to express her anger in an acceptable manner such as: talking, drawing, making up and singing an angry song, banging on drums, punching a punching bag, etc. Creative outlets for anger work very well. The parents should then praise the child for effectively expressing her anger.

It is important to ask the child why she is angry and reinforce that it is all right to be angry. Helping her to express her anger is like medicine because the expression of her anger relieves its destructive force. Emotions that are held in are destructive for all of us. Letting them out is healing and can help prevent *fracturing*. (See Chapter 13)

To Summarize

* Adopted children have two sets of parents both of whom are real.
* Adopted children need to talk about their birth families. Adopted children need to express their feelings.
* Adopted children often confuse (emotionally) their two sets of parents.

Exercise

* Write down your thoughts about the ghosts of the birth family, particularly the natural mother ghost. What emotions come to mind? Write down what you feel about these ghosts. Do you like them, fear them etc? Keep in mind that the ghosts are real people about whom you may know nothing. The way to find out your feelings about the ghosts may well be to find out everything about them. They cannot remain ghosts if you treat them as real.

Experience of the Moment

* You might be experiencing fear right now. Suppose these "ghosts" aren't nice people? Suppose you find out negative things about them? Allow yourself to explore what would happen if you find out bad things. Then think about the anxiety of worrying about these things forever. Would you like to know the answers once and for all and stop the wondering? The constant fear of what you may find adds

up, over the years, to far more anxiety and pain than could be caused by actually dealing with the truth. Tell your inner child that it is safe to explore these emotions and that you will take care of her as always and that both of you are okay.

Chapter 13:

Preventing the Fracture

Prior to age six to eight, the approximate age of cognition, a child doesn't have the ability to truly understand logical process. While the adopted child understands that something earthshaking and sad has occurred, she cannot grasp the concept and what it truly means. She cannot yet look at cause and effect.

Once the child reaches the age of cognition she will play an internal "tape" blaming herself for being given up for adoption and if there is no intervention, a serious *fracturing* of the personality will ensue. Before the *fracture*, the child will be able to talk openly about her rage, pain, sadness and fear as these feelings are accessible at this age. After the *fracture* point, these feelings will be experienced as occurring at the same time. This will cause the feelings to become interwoven with each other, as if intertwined in an entangled ball. The child will not be able to experience one of these feelings without feeling all of them. This is truly overwhelming for the child and to survive, the feelings have to be repressed. Hence, early latency, the years between six to eight, represents a critical therapeutic window of opportunity and it is at this point that a knowledgeable psychotherapist or counselor can make a significant difference. Let us explore how parents and therapists can make the most of this opportunity as well as look at the value of a reunion between the adopted child and her birth family at this time.

One of the most striking events that I see regularly is a room full of adults; adoptees, adoptive parents, prospective adoptive parents and natural parents, all of them articulate in any subject except when they attempt to talk about their adoption experience. They cannot find a way to talk about why they are in the support group meeting.   They don't have a language for their adoption experience since it wasn't talked about earlier in their lives. All adopted people need to develop a language for their adoption experience and if we help the adopted child talk about it while she is

> The language of adoption is a verbal means of expressing one's feelings about one's adoption experience.

growing up, she will not be language deficient when it comes to adoption and she won't have the fears that those who did not learn how to talk about it at an early age have had to overcome as adults.

Myths:
- A child of this age would not be thinking about her birth family.
- A child at this age should never be reunited with her birth family.
- Leave them alone and they will be fine. Don't open up a can of worms.

Facts:
- Children of all ages think about their birth family.
- In general, there is no reason why a child of this age cannot be reunited.

*   No one can successfully deal with the pain of the loss of a mother alone, particularly a child.

Prior to the age of cognition, (six to eight) the adopted child does not truly comprehend what happened to her. She will talk about her feelings rather freely if given the opportunity.

Once the age of cognition is reached it is inevitable that the child, without answers to the questions she has about her beginnings will make up her own answers. Since children think the universe revolves around them, the adopted child's answers to her questions will leave her feeling she is to blame because she believes she is defective and unlovable or she wouldn't have been given up. Once the child comes up with these "bad" answers, she will experience pain, anger, sadness, confusion etc. These emotions will be too powerful and scary to experience and the child will fracture. The fractured

> "...the adoptee who is able to see, touch and feel the natural parent can believe the fact that the person does care, but could not, at the time of the child's birth take care of her." – *The Adoption Triangle*

personality now develops on the foundation of the false belief that the child is indeed unlovable and the "self" is resting on the psychological fault-line of the fracture. This belief in one's unlovability causes feelings that are intolerable to experience or accept and she must then shut down or stop feeling to survive.

If the adoptive parents can intervene and find a way to encourage the child to talk about what she is thinking and feeling, it is very possible to stop the bad answers from being cast in concrete and hence inhibit the onslaught of intolerable feelings leading to the *fracture*. **Hence, this period represents a real therapeutic opportunity and is a critical time**. After the fracture, these feelings will become repressed and intertwined in an entangled ball that is very difficult to unravel.

Several years ago a seven-year-old adopted female was brought to me for a session. She had been having nightmares for years and never woke up, never remembered having them and all her parents could do was hold her while she shrieked in terror until she quieted down. I asked her if her mother had told her I was also adopted? Her eyes opened very large and she said "no", she hadn't. I then asked her if she thought about adoption and she said, "no". Then I asked if she ever thought about her natural mother. She said "sometimes". When I asked her what *sometimes* meant she became very concrete and replied, "about once a week." What do you think about her? I asked. She responded with a barrage of questions, "Who is she? What does she look like? Where is she? Does she think about me? Why didn't she keep me? Does she love me? Is she all right?" and finally, "I have to meet her before I die!" Her mother calls from time to time and reports that she hasn't had a nightmare since our visit. Now, all that really happened in our session was that the adoptee was given the freedom to talk about what was troubling her on the inside. Being able to talk about what happened and ask all the questions may be enough to prevent the fracture. Even without concrete answers, the child gets relief by being able to freely express her feelings and thoughts.

I personally believe that if a reunion at this age can be accomplished (with a great deal of preparation), it can be a blessing for the adopted child, her adoptive family and her birth family. I am often asked wouldn't it be too confusing for a child, having two mothers in her life? Well, it is confusing, but it is more confusing for the adoptee when her natural mother is missing from her life. Don't children of divorce commonly live in a relationship with two mothers?

I think that the best person to convince a child who is on the verge of believing she is unlovable that she is loveable is the child's natural mother. What a priceless treasure that is for the adoptee! If done early enough, the *fracture* will be obviated and the child's life will be remarkably and wonderfully different. Of course, a reunion needs to be done carefully and I highly recommend seeking the advice and counseling of someone very knowledgeable in this area.

To Summarize

* Between the ages of six to eight years there is an opportunity to stop the fracturing of the personality of the adopted child.

* This same age offers a wonderful opportunity for reunion with the birth family, which can be of tremendous benefit for all those whose lives have been affected by the adoption.

Exercise

* Take a moment and think of the terror that you might be aware of in terms of adoption. Then realize that the adopted child, at a young age, has these same terrors and has to cope with them alone, without any support. As adults we need help to understand and survive these feelings. Well, the adopted child didn't (or doesn't) have any help and survived in spite of it all. We need to have empathy for that child for what she went through. Close your eyes and give her a hug and tell her you love her.

Experience of the Moment

* You might be feeling unsafe at the moment. Understand that these feelings about adoption are among the most powerful in the world. If you haven't had help learning to talk about it then you are going to have difficulty with the feelings. The more you can talk about these issues, the more you become desensitized to the topic. Look around you and see that you are physically safe. Say out loud in your head, "Nothing is happening now, I know it feels like it, but I just looked and we are okay. Relax."

Chapter 14:

Beginning to Build
an Authentic Identity

Since adoptees may have been forced to keep their pain, anger and sadness within for so long, adolescence is a time when they may start to express it overtly, acting out in ways that clearly signal they are in trouble. Their parents are more likely to seek psychotherapy for them at this point. Adoptive parents usually feel that their youngster's problems have nothing to do with adoption or that the child's genetic heritage and/or natural mother's actions during pregnancy are to blame. In correcting these mis-perceptions, adoptive parents must be made aware of the special obstacles facing adopted teenagers in achieving the tasks of adolescence and be given guidance in helping their children through this difficult period.

One of the most important actions adoptive parents can take at this stage is to encourage and support their child's desire to connect with her natural mother. The issues, problems, and potential rewards of a search in terms of the adolescent adoptee's developing identity and her relationship with her adoptive parents need to be examined.

While children at earlier stages of development are generally unable to take the healing process into their own hands, adolescents may act on their own to seek help for problems from professionals or other outside sources. Thus, on the assumption that the readership of *Adoption Healing* will include teenagers as well as adults, a section of this chapter will address adolescents directly, dealing with the pros and cons of searching for natural parents and how to broach this issue with adoptive parents. The advisability of family therapy, as well as individual counseling, is also discussed.

Myths:

- Adopted adolescents are no different than their non-adopted peers.
- If the adoptee has problems, it is either non-adoption related or genetic.
- An adopted person, if they must have a reunion, should wait until they are an adult.

Facts:

- Adopted adolescents have their own special set of needs that must be respected.
- Adolescence is the time of identity solidification and for the adoptee is often very painful and confusing.
- A reunion should preferably take place before puberty.

During adolescence, the adoptee is faced with her own sexuality, questions about her own creation and the reality of the confusion of her identity. She wonders who she is, really, and more and more, she wonders who her parents are, particularly the identity of her natural mother. She may start to look at faces on the street, consciously or unconsciously, as a way of searching for someone who looks like her. She may question her own budding sexuality and if she doesn't know her true genetic identity, can she trust her sexual identity?

As the adoptee matures physically, there may be added tension in the household. She can now presumably do what her mother, for example, couldn't do... give birth. Her adoptive mother may be jealous of her and become (unconsciously) antagonistic. Her father may also look at her and get angry for the same reason. Her sexuality may be a slap in the face to her parents, a harsh reminder of what they couldn't do. The adoptee is unlikely to be aware of this, but the tension in the home will surely have its effect on all family members.

The adoptee's pain, anger and sadness, confusing to say the least, is real and understandable and needs to be respected. For the adoptee, it is as if she is an actress who has been dropped into the middle of the wrong movie. What is her real role? Who is she supposed to be? No one will tell her what happened in the beginning of the movie. She has to figure out what to do from now on, without knowing what happened in the past. In many ways she has no foundation to build on and she may develop a real fear of making mistakes in her

> The average adoptee may well be angry at her adoptive parents for having the nerve to not give birth to her. Or she may be angry at her adoptive parents for "stealing" her away from her natural mother. Either way, she probably carries a lot of rage at her adoptive parents for one reason or another. After all, who is safer to be angry at than them?

life. After all, a mistake could get her thrown out, which is what it feels like happened in the very beginning. She might think it's better to let things happen as they will and then she cannot be at fault. How can she finish forming an identity that was purged from the beginning? This is a mostly unconscious conflict.

The adoptive parents, having no way of understanding the inner turmoil of their child, are likely to say that the adoptee's problems have nothing to do with adoption or that the natural parents (child's genetic heritage, or natural parents alcohol or drug use) are to blame. This confusion has everything to do with what happened before adoption. The adoptee has lost her authentic self and is being forced to play varying roles at varying times according to her perception of the wishes of the people around her. She is likely to be acquiescent, a people pleaser with her friends, a grateful daughter, a happy-go-lucky teenager, etc. However, inside, she is confused and needs help.

Adoptees often experience a sense of isolation which arises not only from the difficulties they have in confronting their own feelings but also from the inability to share their emotional reality with significant others – particularly adoptive parents. The adopted person is often afraid of talking about adoption with her adoptive parents. She may be afraid of hurting them or she may have sensed that they didn't want to talk about adoption, ever. The adoptee needs to understand that she cannot hurt her adoptive parents and that adults are in charge of their own feelings. Hopefully her adoptive parents will be supportive, but if they are threatened or saddened by a search, the adoptee can relieve their worries by expressing her true feelings toward them, reassuring them that she is not going to abandon them.

For the most part, an adoptee's search is a search for herself, for completeness, to know her own beginnings. She is not searching because of anything her adoptive parents did or did not do. One would hope that all adoptive parents, because they love their adopted child, would support anything that would make the adoptee more whole, more content and happier. The adoptee does not have to share her search with her adoptive parents, however, there is a down side to keeping the secret If the adoptee

> When a birthmom searches for an adoptee, she is giving a gift. All too often, the adoptees doesn't know how to unwrap it for quite a while.
>
> In the rare instances where a mom turns an adoptee down, She is in all likelihood really saying she cannot cope with her own pain.

does not tell her parents what she is doing, then she is lying by omission and she will have anxiety about the adoptive parents' potential discovery of the search; anxiety that will cause a change in her relationship with her parents. The likelihood is that they will know something is wrong. The adoptee should surely weigh the pros and cons of sharing what she is doing with them. One of the factors for the adoptee to consider is the possibility that her adoptive parents may have all the information that the adoptee needs to complete her search. Adoptive parents often know the original name of the adoptee or the name of her natural mother and perhaps even more information than that.

What are the possible ramifications and benefits of search and reunion for the adoptee?. First of all, one should not just search for one's parents in a vacuum. The adoptee should do a great deal of reading, particularly "Where Are My Birthparents?" a guide to the emotions of the search. A support group should be sought out and meetings attended if at all possible.

Search is a process and the journey is in many ways more important than the results. Six to eight months of support group meetings and reading before embarking on the search would be a reasonable amount of time for getting prepared. A reunion is not a be-all and end-all. It is a beginning of a new way of life, but to take advantage of it, fully enjoy the benefits of it, ongoing work is necessary.

It should be noted that **all** reunions cause pain. The better the reunion, the greater the pain. And anger. And sadness. This is a good thing, not a bad one. Reunion brings the adoptee back to the initial trauma and revisiting the trauma is the only way to heal. Since so much pain is involved in reunion, it is truly necessary to

"I found the best natural parents in the world. They even lived across the street from me when I was a teenager and I didn't know it. They are great. I hurt so bad, seeing what I missed. I love my adoptive parents, but this is not about them. I'm also so angry at them for giving me up." – Female adoptee, aged 32, after a wonderful reunion.

experience some of the pain in preparation for the reunion. Support group meetings and/or individual counseling can help facilitate this process. It is hard to imagine how anyone could not gain from a search and if they are lucky, a reunion. The searcher will always come away ahead of the game as the search is a search for self.

Reunions cause dynamic regression. The natural mother regresses to the age that she was at the time of losing her baby to adoption. The adoptee regresses back to a series of younger personas. Two days old, sixteen years old, two weeks old, seven years old, etc. These changes can occur in an instant. Truly the roller-coaster ride of one's life. This is normal and healthy. It allows the adoptee to mature and heal in some ways that are unavailable without the reunion. This is not to say that the maturing and healing are not possible without reunion, but reunion facilitates the process.

> "Until about 9 months of age, the newborn's experience is a oneness with her mother. A symbiotic existence during which the newborn doesn't even know she is a separate entity. Somehow I connect with that oneness and on a cellular level I remember it. So therefore, I can (as much as possible for a non-mother) feel like I'm on either side of it... Mother's side and baby's side." Female adoptee, age 31

The support group meeting process alone can help the adoptee develop an independent identity and separate from her parents. She can establish a true sense of self and develop comfort with and control over her life and her life course.

Adolescence is the time of the "romance fantasy" discussed in Chapter Six. One of the ways to stop the fantasy is to bring some reality to the theater. By searching and finding and hopefully having a reunion with one's birth family, the adoptee can start to take back parts of her authentic self. This can only happen with a great deal of work, however. These changes are not magically brought about by reunion. They can occur after a tremendous amount of continued support group meetings, reading and perhaps individual counseling.

For the authentic self to be resurrected, the adoptee has to get in touch with all of her feelings, both positive and negative. Only by experiencing her true feelings can she truly experience her true self.

Most people who search will be accepted by their original family. The people who go to support group meetings have an even better chance of getting what they want. As of this writing, of those adoptees who have regularly attended Adoption Crossroads meetings in New York City and let themselves feel all of their feelings, less than six have been ultimately turned down by their mothers since 1986. Unfortunately, those who don't come to meetings get turned down more frequently. Support group meetings are truly a requisite of the search process and highly recommended before, during and after the reunion.

It is important to understand that reunion is a doorway of opportunity for personal growth. Reunion doesn't cause the growth in and of itself, but it does open the door. It is up to those who have reunited to decide if they want to continue their journey of self-discovery.

To Summarize

- Adolescence is a time of turmoil for all teens, but is very often a particularly tumultuous period for an adoptee.
- Searching for and meeting with one's natural parents can help the adoptee to solidify her identity and move forward with her life.
- A reunion is not a panacea. It will not solve anything, but it offers the opportunity for tremendous change with a lot of hard work.

Exercise

- Close your eyes and think about how frightening it might be to meet your mother for the first time as an adult. Then consider how frightening it might be to actually be accepted and loved by your own mother. Why not try to write these feelings and thoughts down in your journal. Most adoptees are just as afraid of being accepted as they are of being turned down by their mothers.

Experience of the Moment

- You might be feeling agitated from the above exercise. It is important to recognize all of your feelings about what you are doing. The process of search and reunion is one of the most brave, challenging and frightening things that any adult can undertake. Getting in touch with all of your feelings as you go along is your safety net. As long as you are in touch with what you are doing, you will be prepared for anything at the end of the journey.

Chapter 15:

Taking Charge of Your Life,
with and without Therapy

The treatment of adult adoptees poses special problems for psychotherapists. The differences between adoptee and non-adoptee clients need to be examined, with particular attention paid to the traps therapists are likely to fall into when treating adoptees. The manner in which therapists can develop the special skills needed to establish trust needs to be explored. Specific techniques and therapeutic images that have proven useful in helping clients access and unravel the intertwined ball of repressed feelings must be examined.

We will look at the precipitating incident that brings the adoptee to therapy; childhood memories, dealing with the fracture and its result, problems in living an authentic life and changing ego states, and we will look at the parallels in treatment of the adoptee with the treatment of abused people.

Therapists also need special knowledge and skills in dealing with clients who are in the process of search and reunion. We will present in depth information on how to prepare and help clients to search for their natural mothers, what to expect when clients have a reunion, and how to help clients integrate this new relationship into their lives.

Events in the adult adoptee's life such as marriage, pregnancy/the birth of a child, or the death of an adoptive parent frequently trigger the surfacing of emotional conflict around adoption. Since the pain, despair, and rage around adoption have been deeply repressed for decades, these emotions are largely inaccessible and potentially whelming. Thus, most adoptees eventually need help – either in the form of psychotherapy and/or support groups – in examining and dealing with their emotions. Nevertheless, there are many ways in which adult adoptees can begin the process of healing on their own. We will focus on steps adoptees can take to minimize the negative effects of adoption on their lives and begin to construct an authentic sense of self.

The first step in dealing with any problem is to acknowledge that there *is* a problem. For many adoptees, even considering this possibility is very difficult. Merely thinking about adoption can raise extremely painful and confusing feelings, some of which seem "crazy" or "bizarre" to the adoptee. Commonly held myths about adoption, natural mothers and their attitudes, the illegality and/or futility of searching for natural parents, etc., convey the message that "dwelling" on their adoption is useless, thus further discouraging adoptees from rocking the boat. These feelings and myths must be dealt with before adoptees can begin to examine the impact of adoption on their lives. It is easy for an adoptee to feel "crazy." She may go through a large part of her life thinking thoughts about herself and her differentness that feel too bizarre to say to another human being.

Growing up in a home without your birth family feels schizophrenic. When you exist in a "crazy" situation and no one will validate it, the tendency is to feel that you are crazy. Lacking the details of the true story of her birth and beginnings, the adoptee often feels that she was zapped into existence, fell from outer space or picked out in the baby store. She feels different from non-adopted people but cannot describe how or why. She is afraid to tell others how she feels for fear of proof of her "craziness." Going to support group meetings, reading and talking to others will help the adoptee understand that she is not alone and her thoughts are not crazy, but normal for someone who has had her experience.

Books provide the most accessible and least threatening avenue through which adoptees, their families and helping professionals can begin to explore the impact of adoption on the adoptee's life. There is a list of recommended books in the back of this work and it is very advisable to start reading as you start the healing process. The books can be used, not only as a source of information about the adoptee's experience, but as a means of gaining insight into the experience of a natural mothers and adoptive parents.

Myths:

- No special knowledge is necessary to treat adoptees in therapy.
- Adoptees have no more need for therapy than anyone else.
- If an adoptee does need therapy, it's probably a genetic thing.

Facts:

- Some special knowledge is needed to treat adoptees successfully.
- People who suffer severe trauma commonly need therapy.
- Adoptees suffered a severe trauma when they were separated from their mothers. Therefore, it is likely that they will need some counseling.

What will drive an adoptee to seek therapy? One of the

triggers (marriage, pregnancy/birth, death of a parent, breakup of a relationship) has usually occurred. The adoptee may present herself to the therapist saying, "I guess being adopted has affected me, but I don't know how" or "I have great (adoptive) parents, so I shouldn't be affected." The adoptee may not even think losing her natural family has anything to do with her life. It may take some time for the adoptee to realize that the effects of the initial separation radiate through most aspects of her life.

One task for the therapist is to determine why the adoptee is coming to therapy now. The adoptee may not consciously know, but if she can figure it out and understand the feelings and thoughts that precipitated seeking some help, it will help her see the connection to her adoption more clearly. The adoptee may very likely avoid the issue.

One trap for professionals is that the adoptee may not raise adoption as an issue or even disclose it at all. She may disclose it and then do her best to deny it's an issue. She may then sidestep the topic at any cost. Keep in mind that the adoptee may well feel that her life depends on **not** talking about adoption at all and certainly not feeling the feelings associated with her experience.

At this point, we should talk about fear of fear. If someone is afraid of feeling some emotion and they allow themselves to get in touch with their fear of feeling that emotion, they may experience to a degree, the very emotion they are trying to avoid. They will therefore be afraid of their fear. This fear of fear is very common in adopted people (as well as others) and can make therapy with the adoptee very difficult indeed.

Since the adoptee did suffer many "wounds," the period of time around the fracture and forward into adolescence may well be repressed. Childhood amnesia, is common for trauma survivors and in my experience working with adoptees, a great number of them have lost their memory of large periods of time of their childhoods.

Any direct pathway to the pain of the *fracture* is likely to be blocked.

The therapist needs to be aware that an adoptee, after disclosing her adoptive status, is likely to present herself much like someone with a dysfunctional family who can't remember her childhood. Here are some of the areas the therapist should explore:

- What was the relationship with her(adoptive) parents like? (The Trap: Many adoptees idealize their adoptive parents to protect themselves from the threat of being disowned by their adoptive parents should the adoptee have "bad" thoughts about them.)
- What kind of intimate relationships has the adoptee had?
- Was the adoptee a good or acting-out adoptee?
- Does the adoptee believe that all babies are loveable?
- Does the adoptee believe that she was evil, deficient or defective?
- How did the adoptee do in school? Many adoptees appear to be learning disabled or to have attention deficit disorder when in fact they are day-dreaming.
- Does the adoptee have a good sense of her own identity and does she know what she wants to do with her life?

The adoptee may not be able to give truthful answers to the above questions because her real feelings have been repressed to survive. Never forget that the adoptee has suffered the psychological death of her mother and she has probably not been able to verbalize or acknowledge this loss in any way. Her body and unconscious mind remembers this loss and therefore the unresolved grief about this loss should be a primary focal point for her therapy.

It is harder to deal with a psychological death than a real one because the adoptee is aware that her natural mother is out there somewhere and the adoptee doesn't know if she is all right or not, alive or dead, happy or sad. Just like someone who is declared missing in action, for the adoptee her mother is also missing; MIA... Missing in Adoption. There is no closure. The adoptee's experience of dealing with this psychological death of her natural mother is schizophrenic. For the adoptee there is no reality. The adoptee was not encouraged to mourn her loss, but to deny it. She is stuck forever at the first stage of mourning.

The adoptee understandably wants the pain to disappear. You can never remove the pain of the death of a loved one, but you can learn how to manage the pain and live with it, if you grieve your losses.

Dealing with the fracture and its effects

The Fracture and Society: Neither the adoptive parents nor society want the adoptee to acknowledge her feelings. To do so would destroy the myth that there is no pain in adoption, that everyone is better off. The adoptee must learn to numb her emotions about her adoption to deal with the excruciating pain that no one else wants to acknowledge, which would in fact help her heal. The interwoven ball or knot of confusing, painful emotions gets more and more tightly woven, making it harder and harder to function as a real person.

At the core of the adoptee's emotions is a giant ball of intertwined, indistinguishable feelings. These feelings terrorize the adoptee because they are so pervasive and interwoven, difficult to separate into individual feelings such as pain, anger and sadness. The adoptee may feel like she is experiencing 17 different feelings at the same time and she won't be able to recognize the individual feelings because they are intertwined, and experiencing the feelings all at once is just too much for anyone to handle. The adoptee has a great deal of rage and unspeakable fear of separation or abandonment as a result of the primal and subsequent wounds and these feelings go down to her core. The therapist should always be looking for the rage and the fears as they will be woven into the emotional fabric of the adoptee.

Rage and Sadness: The adoptee must at some point accept the rage and sadness at what has happened. The following things all feed the rage and sadness:

- The sense that someone is missing or something is wrong. (Well someone is missing, the most important someone of all. Her mother, and what could be more wrong than that?)

- The conflict between the adoptee's two mothers, which has been mentioned earlier.

- Looking in a mirror which, for the adoptee, is confusing indeed. Looking at a face that is not "mirrored" by any other face the adoptee is able to see. Somewhere the question awaits... who do I look like? Where did I get those eyes or that nose? And then inevitably, who is she, where is she and the biggest questions of all, did she love me and why did she give me away?

> "I always thought something was missing, but I didn't know what it was. It was just a sense of emptiness; a general, indistinguishable empty space that I could not explain, nor did I feel capable of talking to anyone about it. I thought if I told someone how I felt, they would think I was crazy. I just had this big hole in my soul and I had no understanding of why it was there until I found the support group where I learned to identify my feelings and express my sadness and anger over the loss of my natural mother. That feeling of being incomplete and empty is now gone. I healed that part of me and I almost forgot that it had ever existed. I would not have ever worked through that feeling if it hadn't been for the support group! That constant low-lying but ever present sense of emptiness, loneliness and pain was one of the worst feelings I have ever had in my life and I am so happy that it is gone forever Julie, 37 year-old adoptee.

•   Dating or getting close to someone puts the adoptee in touch with feelings of impending doom. As an adoptee begins to get close to someone, she begins to feel more and more at risk because she believes, based on her experience of losing her mother, that the person she gets close to will ultimately leave. An adoptee tends to follow one of several patterns as a result of the three traumas. Either she avoids intimacy in the first place, never leaves relationships, no matter how bad, or sabotages relationships, thereby giving her control of the ending.

•   Birthdays have a schizophrenic quality for the adoptee. She is told to be happy on a day which is the reminder of the "death" of her mother. If she says she is not happy, she will most likely be told that she is indeed happy and be asked, "What's the matter with you, Honey? This is your birthday, a happy day." The adoptee is in a bind, another catch-22, if she does and if she doesn't conform. Reality is gone. She is invalidated again and her grief gets buried deeper.

•   Any perceived rejection or abandonment or anything that hints of separation of any kind, such as failed relationships, reading or watching Bambi, or other fairy tales, going to camp, attending the first day of school, death, or just seeing other people who look like their families, may trigger rage and despair for the adoptee. Any one of these or similar events can elicit very strong emotions for the adoptee and the adoptee will generally react by displaying a strong need to cling to others, push others away or, the adoptee may display both behaviors simultaneously.

      The average adoptee won't recognize her anger, pain and sadness or her fear of abandonment because it will bring her to the center of her giant ball of intertwined emotions, the emotions of the Fracture.

In terms of fear of abandonment, the average adoptee can "feel" rejected by a street lamp. The fear of abandonment is so ingrained in the adoptee's personality that it can show up for no apparent reason. The adoptee finishes a phone conversation, hangs up and something within her psyche says the relationship with the person she was just talking to is over. She feels that somehow she did something wrong and has "blown" the friendship. She might then find an excuse to make a check-back call, just to see what kind of reception she gets, hopefully a good one, to prove to herself that she didn't make a mistake and lose the relationship.

The adoptee's difficulty with living an authentic life

"If I don't know experience or understand my feelings, how can I feel that I am real?" "How can I live an authentic life if I don't know my own feelings?" "If I don't feel real, is my life a dream?" These are the questions an adoptee may ask herself. The adoptee cannot live an authentic life without being told the facts of her beginnings. To the average adoptee, everyone else was born but not her. She feels like she was hatched or comes from Mars perhaps. Since the adoptee is cut off from the feelings of the *fracture*, she cannot be true to herself. She knows not what drives her and basically goes through her life "blind" to what is really going on inside.

One of the major tasks of her therapeutic work, whether in a support group or in therapy, is for the adoptee to get in touch with all of the emotions that drive her; all the hidden feelings she has about herself, both of her mothers and the world. As she starts to be able to do this, she starts to become authentic or real in a way she can never be without this process. She starts to "see" the world and experience it rather than just exist in it. This is very difficult work because the hidden feelings are so powerful. This process must be done carefully and with respect for the fear of the fear of all of those most potent emotions.

Because they suffered the trauma of the separation from their natural mothers, it is very common for adoptees to navigate their lives by walking on a tightrope that they cannot see. As is common with trauma victims, the adoptee often feels like the initial trauma is going to happen again. After all, it happened once and she knows not why. To protect herself, she walks the tightrope. But, where does she put her foot next? She thinks and she "knows" she caused the initial disaster, but not how she caused it. She asks herself what she did wrong and how can she avoid doing it again? She must conduct her life in a manner to avoid doing it again. She walks very carefully, always feeling for the tightrope. Living this way, one is always on edge, perpetuating the hyper-vigilance of childhood, always afraid of something going wrong. The adoptee is prone to anxiety attacks and general dis-ease. The adoptee might do well to try the anti-panic attack affirmation offered in Chapter One.

The way out of this dilemma is for the adoptee to gradually, intellectually come to understand that the initial abandonment can never happen again. Once this concept is owned by her logically (not always easy to do), inner child work can be used to change this very painful way of living.

At some point, during the healing process, the adoptee may regress back to a very young age and assume a fetal position and actually appear to herself and to her therapist as a young child. As she gets in touch with her inner child's feelings from infancy, her body and mind take on the persona of that age to which she has regressed. She'll act like a baby and talk (content) like a baby; her voice may even have a baby-like quality to it. During these times, there is the opportunity to do some intense inner child healing, helping the adoptee to know and understand that she is lovable and not at constant risk of suffering a disaster as she assumes. The work that can be done during these regressions is of great value to her journey to wholeness.

There are many psychological parallels between the adopted person and someone who has been sexually, physically or emotionally abused. Simply put, survivors are all the same. Except for the precipitating event, most survivors have the same difficulties to overcome; the same lack of feeling lovable, frequent feelings of being at risk, free-floating anxiety, difficulty with relationships, etc. The cause is different and the work is different, but the "symptoms" are very similar. Important to keep in mind always is the profound nature of the wound and the respect that must be given to the difficulty of the healing process. All adoptees need to be treated as if they just had an accident and are now in the emergency room. Just as a victim of an automobile accident who is in shock may well deny the need for treatment, so too the adoptee is most often unaware that she is wounded, let alone aware of the depth of the wound. The adoptee needs to approach the healing journey with caution, understanding that she will awaken some powerful and scary emotions. Much can be done to change the way the adoptee is affected today by her tragic experience of losing her natural family early in her life, if the work is done slowly, at a pace that is comfortable for her.

Here are a few ways of approaching the locked closet full of scary emotions:

The adoptee imagines an orange. Inside is the interwoven fabric of emotions, the unspeakable ball of pain from the separation and loss of mommy. All strands of this ball of pain are woven together. Inside the orange, they are safely contained. The orange ball has a small door with a huge padlock, which can only be opened when both therapist and patient are in agreement. The knob of the door is so big that even with the padlock off, a tiny finger pressure will help keep it closed. The therapist explains that adoptee's emotions are all confused and intertwined, so that it is difficult to understand her feelings. The adoptee removes the padlock but keeps her finger on the door, just in case. Keep a check on how the adoptee is feeling. No strand is so powerful that it cannot be safely examined. The adoptee pulls out a strand of feeling and examines it. The adoptee is asked what feeling the strand represents. The therapist explains that every time she does this, it reduces the power of what is left in the orange. The therapist reassures the adoptee that she will never pull out or experience anything she can't handle. This helps to put the adoptee in charge of her emotions.

Alternatively, the adoptee imagines a gum ball machine filled with many different colored gum balls. Each color of gum ball represents a different feeling. The gum ball machine is built so that only one gum ball comes down at once. Another cannot come out until the first one is examined. The adoptee proceeds as above, using substituting the gum ball for the strands inside the orange.

Doing this work with the gum balls or the orange ball will help the adoptee start to understand that she will not perish or disintegrate if she feels her true feelings. She will be well on her way to taking charge of her own life and she will finally be truly **living**.

To Summarize

- The experience of being separated from her mother radiates through every aspect of the adoptee's life.
- By helping the adoptee experience her feelings and then understand why she feels the way she does, the door opens to changing the way her experience affects her life.

Exercise

- Close your eyes and try to imagine either the gum ball or the ball of interwoven emotions. At random, let a gum ball drop into the chute or take a thread of emotion. What emotion does the thread or gum ball represent? Write down in your journal all that you can about the emotions or thoughts generated by the gum ball or thread.

Experience of the Moment

- You might be experiencing a lot of anxiety about now. Taking the gum ball or thread out and examining it can be a very powerful experience. As scary as they might be, these are only feelings. Look around you to see that nothing is happening now. Say that out loud in your head, "Nothing is happening now, it only feels like it, and we're okay." Take a deep breath and say the word, "RELAX" out loud in your head. You should now be feeling better. Please note that while the emotions are very strong, you have indeed survived. The emotions did not hurt you. You just experienced them. Next time you experience them, it will be somewhat easier and less scary.

Part Three:

Toward
Healthier Adoptions

Part Three is a wish-list for healthy adoptions and adoptees, including the advisability of open adoption and of regular mental health checkups with a professional throughout the child's development. The purpose of checkups is similar to that of dental checkups, i.e., to nip problems in the bud. These checkups give the therapist an opportunity to see how the attachment process with the adoptive parents is proceeding and to provide the child with a chance to express difficult and confusing feelings before they become repressed.

Chapter 16:

A Wish List

1) Every effort should be made to keep the birth family intact, and if that is not possible, the next choice should be to keep the baby within the extended birth family, always with the priority of ensuring that the baby will be in a safe and nurturing environment.

2) All adoptions should be open adoptions from the beginning. "Open" means regular visits with the natural mother throughout childhood and adolescence, with the proviso that the child is always safe and never at risk. Supervised visits, if necessary, are preferable to none at all.

Myths:

- Children don't need to know where they come from.
- Having regular contact with the birth family would be confusing and destructive to the adopted child and her family.

Facts:

- Every person needs to know the truth of their origins.

- Regular contact with the birth family is less confusing than no contact and will reduce many of the pains and problems that face the adopted person as she lives her life.

3) The child should never be stripped of her name and heritage. Her birth name should be maintained unless there are extenuating circumstances. Children of divorce often maintain their original names, why not the adoptee?

4) The child should have adoption *checkups* periodically throughout her developmental stages to curtail problems as they arise. The focus of the checkups would be to (a) see how the attachment process with adoptive parents is proceeding; (b) allow the therapist to ask some pointed questions about the child's thoughts and fantasies; (c) to observe interactions between parents and the child. Checkups should occur: – within the first month, – at year one, – at one and a half years, – at two years, – after age of discovery, – middle and end of Oedipal stage, – at age of cognition (approximately six to eight years of age); a few sessions at this point, allowing the child to talk about her feelings and thoughts will minimize what gets repressed. If it's a closed adoption, this is the time to open it. Search will minimize the effects of the missing self and will make developmental tasks easier. Knowing two mothers is confusing but not as much as knowing one and fantasizing about the other. At the first sign of pubescence; if the search hasn't started earlier, it should certainly be initiated (always with the child's permission and participation) along with some counseling and then perhaps some short–term therapy during adolescence.

> " The separation of mother and child causes psychic shock and should never occur unless there is no other choice. The wound makes the infant feel that part of itself has disappeared, leaving it with a feeling of incompleteness or lack of wholeness." – *The Primal Wound*

These *checkups* should be seen as similar to trips to the dentist for preventative measures – not as signs that something is wrong or that the child is somehow broken or damaged. Obviously, if "cavities" develop, they should be filled. For the most part, the more the child is allowed to have contact with her birth family and the more the child engages in conversation about the adoption and her feelings, the more likely she will be a happier adoptee, with fewer problems.

To Summarize

- Openness, honesty, truth and preservation of family ties will promote a happier, more well-adjusted adopted individual.

- Regular visits to a therapist well-versed in adoption issues will ward off many of the problems faced by adoptive families.

Exercise

- Close your eyes and try to imagine what it would be like growing up knowing two mothers. Write down your thoughts and feelings in your journal.

Experience of the Moment

- You might be experiencing some conflicting feelings right now. It might seem confusing to think about growing up knowing two moms. Well, it probably would be, but see if you can get in touch with the feelings of not knowing the first mom at all. These are only feelings, and confusing as they might be, they are feelings from the past and can be dealt with best by *not* pushing them away. You may want to repeat the anti-anxiety affirmation from the end of Chapter One at this time.

Part Four:

Getting Help

Obviously, adoptees are not immune to the pressures that motivate non-adoptees to enter therapy or join support groups. On the contrary, because of the profound disruption adoption can have on the development of self, the capacity for intimate relationships, and the ability to live authentic lives in general, adoptees in particular can benefit from therapy **with a skilled practitioner who is knowledgeable about adoption issues**. For a number of reasons, finding such a therapist can be difficult. Chapters 17 and 18 discuss the reasons for these difficulties and make suggestions for locating the right person.

Search and support groups offer an alternative method of healing. Chapter 19 discusses the benefits of joining a group and describes what you might expect from such a group.

Chapter 17:

Choosing the Right Therapist

Unfortunately, the vast majority of psychotherapists lack the skills to address the problems faced by adoptees. Since adoptees are likely to believe adoption is not an issue for them, or often do not even mention that they are adopted, it is easy for therapists to miss adoption-related dynamics.

> "If your therapist is supportive, open to your questioning and doesn't try to force answers on you, then you can feel confident... Above all, trust your own sense of who you are and what your experiences have been. If the healing process is about anything, it's about learning to trust yourself, your feelings, your reality."
> – *The Courage to Heal*

More importantly, an adoptee's experience directly challenges much of what therapists have been taught professionally. It also attacks other deeply entrenched, often unconsciously held assumptions. An adoptee's existential experience is completely different from that of a non-adoptee and therapists (unless they are adopted and have done their own adoption healing) have little in their own experience to draw on as a means of relating to adopted clients. To further complicate the process, if the therapist is an adoptive parent, she may have an unconscious vested interest to not acknowledge the destructive impact of surrender/adoption on the psychosocial development of a child, as she would have to comprehend and acknowledge the consequences of adoption on her own child.

Here we will offer suggestions on how to pick a therapist familiar with or sensitive to adoption-related issues. Although very few therapists specialize in this area, experience in other related fields, such as post-traumatic stress disorder, early mother-child separation and grief work, should make it more likely that a therapist will have the necessary skills and perspective to deal with adoption trauma. Readers are also warned to avoid certain obvious pitfalls, such as going to a therapist who discounts adoption as an issue.

Myths:

- Any good therapist should be able to adequately help an adoptee in therapy.
- Adoptees, if they grew up in a good family, shouldn't need therapy. If they seek therapy, it is not due to losing their natural family.

Facts:

- Special understanding of adoption issues is necessary to be an effective therapist for an adoptee.
- It is likely that all adoptees could use some good counseling, not because there is something is wrong with them, but because the effects of the separation of mother and child are profound and yet well disguised.

Anyone considering getting professional help has the right to interview potential therapists in order to be able to select one suitable for their needs. The prospective client has a right to know where and when the therapist got her degrees, whether or not she is licensed by the state, what specialized training she has had and whether she can accept insurance. The prospective client has a right to know how much experience the therapist has in working with adoption related issues, whether the therapist has personal experience in adoption and what kind of experience she has had. The prospective client should ask for a curriculum vitae from the therapist and also ask what adoption related literature the therapist has read. If the prospective therapist is not forthcoming with this information, the client might well look elsewhere.

There are therapists who, with no experience whatsoever in adoption, have an great deal of sensitivity to the issues. If you are fortunate enough to find one who is sensitive to the issues and feel comfortable with her, she may well be able to help you on your journey.

If you are having difficulty finding a therapist that is right for you, there are several steps you can take. 1) Call your local Department of Social Services and ask them for referrals, 2) call your local hospital and ask for the outpatient social services department, 3) join and adoption search and support group and ask the members for referrals.

To Summarize

- It is likely that anyone involved in adoption could benefit from talking with a therapist about with the effects of their adoption experience.
- A special understanding and sensitivity to adoption issues is necessary for anyone to be an effective therapist for those affected by adoption.
- It is your right to interview prospective therapists until you find one who is right for you.

Chapter 18:

From the Therapist's Perspective:

Unless there are signs indicating otherwise, the adoptee should be treated as someone who has Post Traumatic Stress Disorder. The loss of her mother at the beginning of her life was a trauma of the highest order and needs to be respected as such.

What is different about treating adoptees?

1) Unless the therapist is alert, she may miss the fact that adoption is an issue, or even that her client is adopted.

> If a therapist was abused or abandoned in some way in her childhood and if the therapist has not dealt with her own issues, she will likely be unable to tolerate the intense pain of her client and therefore be ineffective as a therapist.

2) The adoptee is likely to resemble any other person with a dysfunctional family (or any other survivor) who my not be able to recall her childhood.

3) Adoptees often say, "Adoption is not an issue," and many

therapists accept this. It cannot *not* be an issue and must be explored.

Myth:

•   No special knowledge is needed to treat adoptees, they are just like anyone else.

Facts:

•   Special knowledge is needed to treat adopted people since the psychology of the adoptee is different.

---

4) The adoptee and the abused patient parallel one another's experience, although the adoptee has not been "abused" in the usual sense. The effects of the primal wound and subsequent *fracture* are so profound that adopted people should be considered *survivors,* similar to those who have been abused.

5) Adoptees are forced to remain stuck at the first stage of mourning (i.e., denial) – the natural mother has "died" but the adopted child is not permitted to mourn. There is no closure.

6) There is a double-bind, a schizophrenic quality to an adoptee's life. My natural mother is dead, she's not dead; I was born, but I wasn't born; birthdays are a happy time, they are a sad time.

7) There is a special unreal quality to an adoptee's feelings. Because her feelings are intertwined in a giant ball of undistinguishable emotions, the adoptee has great difficulty separating her emotions, or even experiencing them.

8) Adoptees experience special difficulties in living an authentic life.

9) It is more difficult to get an adoptee to trust the therapist and to believe that the therapist can understand and empathize – **because the therapist often can't** empathize and may not want to.

(a) The adoptee's experience attacks much of what therapists have learned professionally, as well as many deeply held assumptions. If the therapist doesn't want to believe what's written here, she needs to ask herself why. Many adoptees do not want to believe the *primal wound* theory – probably most of those involved in adoption don't want to believe it, either.

(b) Many therapists are adoptive parents who have not dealt with their own feelings of infertility. Moreover, therapists are like adoptive parents to their clients anyway, so transference is really going to be difficult for clients. (The conflict between two mothers when the therapist flips back and forth, representing these mothers, is enormous.) The therapist is more likely to experience a strong counter-transference as well, even if she isn't an adoptive parent, compounding the difficulty of working with the adoptee.

10) An adoptee's existential experience is totally different from that of a non-adoptee. Therefore, the therapist often has no idea of and cannot imagine what her client's inner world even looks like.

11) If being adopted is like being from Mars, reunion is like living on Jupiter. Reunion raises the surrealistic quality of the adoptee's life exponentially. In the post-reunion stage, the client's ego states change faster than the second hand on a clock. The adoptee's regressive states may change *so* fast that the therapist can't keep up.

12) If a reunion between the adoptee and her mother is being considered, the therapist will be working with someone who is meeting her mother consciously for the first time. There is nothing

in the therapist's training or the client's life experience to prepare either of them for this event.

13) The therapist must accept the concept that the best way for the adoptee to achieve closure is through (a carefully prepared) reunion.

14) The therapist should also help the client find a support group if possible. Many adoptees have never knowingly talked to another adoptee and may be petrified to do so. A support group environment will very likely be healing in and of itself.

15) The therapist might do well to attend support group meetings, do extensive reading of adoption related literature and attend adoption conferences to truly begin to grasp the work that needs to be done with any client who has been affected by adoption.

To Summarize

- The experience of those involved in adoption is extra-ordinary and any therapist wishing to work with triad members would be well advised to do a great deal of "homework" before attempting to help clients touched by adoption.

Chapter 19:

Finding a Support Group

Adoptees have often spent much of their lives trying to repress the feelings they have around their adoption, so many have never talked to anyone, particularly other adoptees, about their experience. Like AA or other groups organized around a shared problem, adoption support groups provide an opportunity for adoptees to explore these feelings with others who can relate to them in ways that non-adoptees, even skilled therapists, cannot. (You might want to go back and read the **Welcome** chapter at the beginning of this book to get the flavor of a support group meeting.

> "A good support group should be a safe and respectful space in which each member is valued... You should feel accepted and able to speak honestly about your experience and your feelings... The focus should be on each member's individual and unique healing journey." – *The Courage to Heal*

Many support groups are open to all members of the adoption triad, that is, adoptees, natural parents, and adoptive parents. The opportunity to interact with natural mothers, as upsetting as this can initially be, is invaluable for an adoptee attempting to understand her own natural mother's motivation and feelings about surrendering her. Of course, not just adoptees, but all triad members can benefit enormously from a support group comprised of all individuals whose lives have been affected by adoption.

Search and support groups are a source of practical help in dealing with adoption-related issues. Support group help is a necessity for those attempting to search for natural parents or surrendered children, providing assistance in both the difficult logistics of search and the often whelming emotional impact of the search and reunion process.

Adoption search and support groups have sprung up all over the country, even in many smaller communities. This chapter discusses the benefits and experience of participating in one of these support groups.

Myths:

*   Anyone who attends a support group is weak.
*   Support groups are like therapy.
*   Support groups are like a club.

Facts:

*   Only strong people go to support groups.
*   Support groups are not like therapy, though they are supposed to be therapeutic.
*   Support groups are not clubs. They are comprised of individuals with common goals and experiences that bring them together to help or support each other.
*   Support group attendance is the most important action anyone involved in a search can take. The search is the

easy part. Dealing with the emotions is the hard part.

Most adoption support groups are based in peoples' homes and do not have listings in the phone book. Contact your local United Way or Self-Help Clearing House and ask them if they know of any groups in your area. Also, your local library may also be able to refer you to local support groups.

Searching on the Internet for support groups may also be effective. While the chat groups on the Internet may be very helpful, they are not a substitute for in-person support group meetings.

Support groups are not a substitute for therapy and therapy does not obviate the need for a support group. Participating in both therapy and a support group at the same time is synergistic meaning that the benefits of the two together are much more powerful than the benefit of either one of them individually. A support group offers the opportunity to be with others who have shared a common experience and who can be empathetic in a way those who haven't shared the experience cannot.

A support group offers the opportunity for tremendous change and healing. For the most part, if you continually have a safe place like a support group to express your pain, anger and sadness, you will be less anxious, less likely to get depressed and better able to handle the difficulties that life presents to you. This is one of the many hidden benefits of letting out or expressing your hidden feelings. After you have been doing this work for a while, if you do get depressed, excluding clinical depression, there are a few choices that you can make. You can choose to stay depressed and be miserable. You can choose not to be depressed. Saying out loud in your head, which is a way of talking to your unconscious mind, that you refuse to be depressed will often work. The third choice is to stay depressed but to enjoy it. Put on an old favorite sweater or robe, pick a favorite book to read or movie to watch or music that you would like to hear. Make yourself a special meal perhaps. Treat yourself (and your inner child) exactly the way you would want to be treated as a child who doesn't feel good. Mother yourself. Try it. You'll probably like it!

To Summarize

- Support group meetings are the most important part of your search.

- Support group meetings and therapy enhance each other and will help you heal faster than participating in either one without the other.

Exercise

- Try to imagine going to a support group meeting. What feelings come up for you? Try writing your responses in your journal.

Experience of the Moment

- You might be feeling afraid, even petrified of going to a meeting. Most people are very frightened the first time. Don't forget that everyone at the meeting will be in the same boat; everyone has had a similar experience. In fact, a support group meeting will likely feel like the safest place in the world. It's a place where *you* will be understood, perhaps for the first time.

Part Five:

The Challenge to Heal

Most adopted people grew up in homes where talking about one's pain, anger or sadness about adoption was not allowed. This taboo on discussing adoption was often non-verbal or indirect. If that was the case, then those adoptees do not know the language of adoption, do not have a way of expressing their experience. The first step in healing the fracture is to develop a language that will allow you to describe your feelings and thoughts about your experience. For the most part we are not talking about feelings that have to do with adoption, but rather we are talking about feelings that have to do with losing one's natural family.

It is very common for an adoptee to be unaware of any feelings about her experience, or perhaps just be aware of a feeling of unrest. Being numb is a way of avoiding pain. It may serve the adoptee very well when

"Whether we notice it or not, adoption is the window through which we view the outside world. If we honor the child-like part of ourselves, we see that window, take time to open it, and require fewer Band-Aids to repair the damage of just trying to plow through it as if it doesn't exist." – *The Bridge Less Traveled*

she is young, but as adults, we need to feel our feelings to truly live life. If we grew up being afraid of our feelings, then we need to learn that they will not kill us. We will not be annihilated by our feelings. It may feel that way at first, but over time we can learn that we will not die from feeling our real feelings. We need to learn that it is okay to be angry and express it; that it is okay to be sad and express it; that it takes courage to cry... it's not a sign of weakness. Although it feels like it, if we do let ourselves cry, we will not cry forever and our hearts will not break from the pain.

Imagine, once again, that you go to the doctor because you have a terrible, terrible pain in your belly (and you are afraid it is fatal just because you feel it). The doctor says, "Relax, it is just indigestion, take some Maalox." The pain will be the same but your experience of the pain is lessened tremendously and, you become unafraid. So it is with our fear of our emotions. As you learn **what** you feel and **why**, the way you experience your feelings changes and your fear lessens. Eventually you can actually stop being afraid of your feelings and then the whole world changes for you. Imagine, if you will, **not** being afraid of your own feelings!

Some adoptees are aware of feeling something but are unable to describe what they feel. You need to start slowly to examine your inner self. A support group works best for this type of change. You need to try out different words for the feelings and see if they fit. This may take some time. Bear in mind that you may believe that it is wrong to feel anger or sadness, that it is disrespectful or "not nice" or you just *should not*. The fact is that feelings should not be judged as right or wrong. Feelings just are, and you need to be able to identify them and say them out loud.

Imagine, if you will, that you go to the doctor and she asks you why you are there. You reply that you hurt and she asks where you hurt and you say you don't know. Or you say you hurt in your stomach and she asks you to describe your pain and you say you can't. Your doctor wouldn't be able to help you much because you would be lacking a vocabulary to talk about physical pain.

When you say your feelings out loud, they become real, for the first time. When the feelings become real, you can start to understand why you feel what you feel; and when you understand why you feel what you feel, you can start to change the way your experience affects you.

Real healing can only be done when you know where you hurt, why you hurt, and the extent of the pain. You must not make light of the pain, anger and sadness of losing your natural family. If you make light of what happened, you tend to put on Band-Aids and Band-Aids do not solve problems, they just cover them up.

It is important to bear in mind that you lost the most sacred relationship that can ever exist and that it is okay to experience strong feelings about your loss.

If your original parents died in a car crash when you were a few days old, and if you were therefore raised by relatives, everyone would acknowledge that you started your life in a very sad way. You would have pictures and a grave to visit, and you would be allowed and even encouraged to express your sad feelings and your anger. However, as soon as we plug in the word adoption, most people do not see the loss as severe or even a loss at all. However, from the child's point of view, the experience is the same: The loss of one's mother is just the same as a physical death. When there is a psychological death, it is just as sad, just as tragic and needs to be mourned just as much, if not more. To deny this is to deny reality and prohibit grieving, and grieving is an important part of healing.

If you are a typical adoptee, you don't feel safe in the world, you often feel vulnerable, and you may experience panic attacks from time to time. It doesn't take much in today's world to make us feel as if our first loss is happening again. This feeling of reliving our loss of our mother at birth is one of the marks of a trauma survivor.

Since we didn't have words then, we usually do not know what we are feeling when we are having a panic attack. We are just scared to death. We need to know what to say to ourselves when we feel some of these emotions, some of the most powerful emotions in the world.

Most adoptees believe that they were given up because there was something wrong with them. If you were given up then you were defective and the defect was that you were unlovable. (The cause of the *fracture*.) The personality of the adoptee is based on this **false** belief. To heal we must correct this false belief system.

The first step for healing the fracture is for the adoptee to understand the concept that nothing can make a baby unlovable. The adoptee must truly have the intellectual understanding of this fact. Then and only then, once that knowledge is firmly implanted intellectually, the adoptee can take the next step for her healing by learning to believe in her lovability on an emotional level. Once the adoptee is ready for this emotional step, she can do and say the following to herself: Imagine your younger self in your mind, picture that young child that you were and say **out loud** in your head, "You are lovable. Losing your mother wasn't about you, although I know it feels like it. It wasn't about you and you are lovable and deserving. We are both okay." Look around you while you are saying this to prove to you and your inner child that you both are okay, that nothing is happening to you in the real world. (You must absolutely believe, intellectually, that the above statements are true because you can never lie to your inner child.)

If you start to have a panic attack or feel unsafe, say **out loud** in your head: "Nothing is happening now, I know it feels like it, but we're safe. RELAX." Don't forget to look around you while you say this to prove to both your inner child and yourself that nothing is indeed happening.

You will learn how to communicate better and better with

your inner child and you will learn other things to say to your inner child to feel better. We will teach you how to use visualizations, create a "safe place" that you can go to whenever you wish – a very inexpensive vacation on demand. This safe place can be a home base for working with your inner child. You may find that your inner child may "wish" to come home and live with you and there can be a great benefit to this type of re-parenting..

You will be dealing with some very primitive, powerful feelings and you may be afraid that you can't handle these feelings, but you **will** learn to master them.

Bear in mind that in order to heal you must go back and *experience* what happened at the beginning of your life. That way you will know exactly what really happened, what you survived and you will have a new awareness of the strength you had to survive.

In the ensuing chapters you will:

Learn how to channel anger.

Learn affirmations: things to say to yourself (your inner child) out loud in your head in times of need

Make lists of everything that you are angry about, sad about etc.

Recognize that crying is not feeling sorry for yourself, rather, that it is feeling sorry about something sad that happened to you.

Recognize that you have to mourn your losses. Recognize that your losses have not been respected.

Learn to have respect for your own fears and feelings.

Learn to make "I feel" statements.

Find people to talk to who will not challenge what you feel.

You cannot heal if you downplay what happened. You must recognize the full extent of your wounds to be able to clean them out completely.

Your healing can be likened to Emotional Root Canal. It has to be done, is painful, but it is often the only road to good health.

Chapter 20:

Healing the Inner Child:
An Innovative Approach

"When a child's feelings are repressed, especially the feelings of anger and hurt, a person grows up to be an adult with an angry hurt child inside of her. This child will spontaneously contaminate the person's adult behavior."[8]

I've had many teenage adoptee clients who came to me believing that they are broken and need to be fixed and it is so easy (because it is true) to tell them that they are not broken, but their situation is very "broken". So I help them revise the way they think about their situation. This revision is the key to inner child work.

So much of an adoptee's experience had to be repressed because of the three traumas.[9] It

> "Three things are striking about inner child work: the speed with which people change when they do this work; the depth of that change; and the power and creativity that result when wounds from the past are healed." – *Homecoming* – John Bradshaw

had to be repressed for the adoptee to survive the pain, anger and sadness of the reality of her losses. Inner child work offers an effective and less time-consuming method for grieving, healing and recovering as much as possible from the losses that were endured

---

[8] John Bradshaw, *Homecoming: Reclaiming and Championing Your Inner Child*

[9] The three traumas are the primal wound, the discovery of being adopted and the solidification of the belief that one is unlovable.

in childhood. I find that inner child work is faster and therefore less expensive than traditional therapies. Recognizing that the term *inner child* sounds like "psychobabble" or "shrink-speak" and there will surely be some skepticism about this work, I offer the following: When someone is having a temper-tantrum, I hope it is obvious that they are acting like a two year old. What is really happening is that their two year old self (inner child) has taken control of the adult's behavior. Try to tell the adult that she is acting like a two year old and she will get even angrier and deny it.

Your inner child is a representation of the feelings, thoughts and emotions from various times in your childhood. Each of us has many inner children representing different experiences or moments in our past. An inner child is not burdened by the adult teachings and expectations of the outside world. She has emotions and feelings that are the true raw feelings of our younger self and this is where the adult will begin to learn about the feelings that are held deep inside her, within her inner child. Your adult self needs to know that the inner child is her at a younger age, with all the feelings, playfulness and naivete that existed when she was young. Have you ever said, "Relax" inside your head during a difficult time and had it calm you down? If you have done this, you've done inner child work.

Since so many of our pains and anxieties of today are based on painful childhood events that were never resolved, finding ways to "talk" to that hurt child that you were offers a wonderful opportunity for healing. Inner child work is a way to gain access to your unconscious mind and change the way you think about yourself. Much of your adult difficulties come from false beliefs that are the result of a child's way of understanding things. Understanding that children blame themselves for the bad things that happen to them, you can realize that the solution to many of your adult woes is to help your inner child remove the self-blame.

Inner child work does take some practice. I refer the reader to **What We May Be** and **Homecoming** to assist in the ability to do inner child work.   Both of these works are listed in the recommended reading section in Appendix H, along with many other good books on inner child work. My intent here is not to reinvent the wheel, but rather to explain inner child work as it relates to an adoptee's healing path and present some tools and examples of inner dialogue that are particularly helpful for bringing healing to adopted people.

Myths:

- Inner Child work is "psychobabble."
- There is no such thing as an inner child.

Facts:

- An Inner Child is a concept, a way of looking at and communicating with our unconscious minds.
- All human beings have many inner children of different ages.

Before you continue to read this chapter, please go back and read the Proceed with Caution page in the beginning of this book. If you are in therapy, please consult your therapist before doing this work.

It is important as you do this work that you remember the child that you were and find compassion and respect for her. In that way, you can always respect your inner child. Respect the hurt, anger, and sadness of that child. It is important that you treat her well and be on 24 hour call for her. Let her act the way she wants when you are with her. If she is angry and wants to scream, let her do so. If she wants to bang pots and pans, that's great. Always encourage her to feel her feelings, knowing she is safe and will not be punished for doing so because you will be "parenting" her now, parenting her well. Parenting in this sense is treating your inner child the way she should have been treated by her parents.

To begin with, study the basic visualization techniques in Chapter 22. Go to your safe place, then let yourself float back and see yourself at an early age when you were in need of some support and comfort. Walk into the picture, right in front of your young self and, out loud in your head, say, "Hi!" Ask her how she is feeling. She may not want to talk to you. Tell her she can trust YOU more than anyone else in the world. Develop a trusting relationship with her by talking to her out loud in your head many times a day. Be patient with her. She probably hasn't been able to trust anyone enough to talk to about these feelings for a long time. It's okay for her to take time to trust you. Whatever she does or says is okay and keep telling her so.

You must intellectually understand anything you tell your inner child, e.g., it wasn't anything about her that caused her to be given up. If you don't intellectually believe what you say to your inner child, she won't believe it either. Only by telling her the truth can you help her see the truth... the truth that whatever happened to her was not her fault.

All of the visualization techniques and affirmations given in this book lend themselves to inner child healing. You will need to develop your own communication with your inner child. She knows what she needs more than anyone else. If you ask her, she'll tell you. Listen to her and honor her wishes, respect her pain and help her as best as you can. Do not forget that she was the victim. She is not to blame for anything that happened to her. She only deserves empathy.

Two of the most important conversations with your inner child are the following:

1) The Lovability affirmation. Say out loud in your head (to your seven-year-old self), "You are lovable. I know it doesn't feel that way. What happened to you wasn't your fault. We're okay." Tell her she is lovable often. Give her a hug. Tell her you love her. Tell her you are on 24 hour call. Don't leave her without asking her if it's okay to leave, that you will be back shortly. Do this over and over, as often as possible. (Four times an hour, every waking hour for a month should produce a very noticeable change.)

2) The Anti-panic/Anti-anxiety affirmation. When feeling panicked, look around the room to verify that nothing is happening and then say out loud in your head, "It's not happening now, I know it feels like it but it's not. Relax. Calm down. I am here. We're safe."

The adoptee may alter the affirmations to suit her and to fit different occasions. She needs to make a point of visiting her inner child many times a day. Plan activities with her. (See Appendix F of this book for a list of activities for you and your inner child.) It only takes a few seconds, but she will feel so much better. Anytime something is upsetting for the adoptee and she cannot figure out what's wrong or why she is feeling the way she is, she can ask her inner child to tell her what is wrong. She will probably get an accurate answer and then she, the adult, can deal with it.

What you are doing is giving your inner child good parenting. Treating her today the way she should have been treated in the past, honoring her feelings and her true self. This *will* carry forth and help both of you come to an inner peace that you have never known. One day you and your inner child may stop being afraid of anything at all, you may be totally without fear. This state is attainable with the work outlined here. Hard work to be sure, but when you are no longer afraid of your feelings you will be truly free. What an enormous gift you will have given yourself!

Someone who has been denied their feelings has likely

become a prisoner of her pain and has become adept at unconsciously avoiding the triggers for her pain.   This is understandable because the pain is so pervasive. Once you become practiced at your inner child work and let your pain be experienced, embraced as part of your healing, you will be set free and no longer a prisoner.

> "If I stop being angry at my natural mother I will lose her. It's all I have of her and I don't want to give it up." Female adoptee, age 16

Also, you need to recognize that change is often scary. Healing certainly involves pain, anger and sadness. Adoptees, for example, know exactly how to deal with feelings of rejection. They are experts at it and it fits like an old cramped shoe that they don't want to throw away. You might want to make a list of what you are afraid of changing and why. What will really happen if you give up your pain, anger and sadness? What can you put in its place? It's time to be creative!

To Summarize

- Inner child work is a way of easing and resolving some of the pains and hurts of childhood.
- You can do inner child work on your own after some initial guidance.
- You can gain inner peace through this work.

Exercise

- Close your eyes and try to imagine what it would be like if were never again to be afraid of anything. Relish it and know that you can attain that state of being.

EXPERIENCE OF THE MOMENT

- You might be experiencing some happiness at these comforting thoughts ... Enjoy the experience.

Chapter 21:

Anger

Anger is one of a human being's most basic emotions. Babies will show extreme anger (rage) on the first day of life. If they are removed from the breast or bottle before they are ready, they make tiny little fists, turn red in the face and howl with rage. This a normal and healthy response.

Myths:

- Anger is a terrible thing.
- People who say they are angry are angry people.

Facts:

- Anger is not a terrible thing. What you do with it may indeed be terrible.
- When someone says they are angry, that does not mean they are an angry person, it means they are angry about something and expressing it which is a healthy thing to do.

As we grow up, we are supposed to learn how to manage our anger, how to express it in societally approved ways. Unfortunately many people do not learn how to do this. They either learn to stuff their anger or express it in ways that are hurtful. Anger that is unexpressed is always going to have an effect on us. If we don't say it out loud, then we will act-it out (hurting those around us) or act-it in, thereby hurting ourselves. Unexpressed, bottled up anger will most likely cause one to sabotage relationships, push people away, cause psychosomatic illnesses, do bad things to one's body or any combination of the above. Having anger is not bad, but it is essential to learn how to recognize it, acknowledge it and express it in a healthy manner. Anger is just one letter short of danger and if we don't know how to deal with the emotion it can be very dangerous indeed.

> "In reference to body pain, talk to your body. Tell it, "I will take care of you. I need you to cooperate with me, instead of fighting me and we will both feel better."
> – Julie, 37 year-old adoptee.

Anger is like toxic waste, but it is recyclable. Among other things, one can lessen or release anger by channeling it. To channel it, you need only say a few quick words out loud in your head. You do **not** have to feel it, or even know why it is there. You need to say, for example: I'm going to take my anger and use it to *exercise* or I'm going to take my anger and use it to *paint,* etc. Common activities that lend themselves to channeling are: doing your daily work, cleaning, doing the dishes, exercising, mowing the lawn, jogging, painting, playing music, walking, writing poetry, prose or music. Any physical activity will be useful to channel your anger. Although it may be tempting, you cannot channel your anger into reading a book, watching TV or listening to music. Sedentary activities just won't cut it. You may need to say (again, all of this is out loud in your head) I'm going to take my anger and use it to get up out of this chair (a jump start) and clean the house.

The more you channel, the better you will feel, the less

anger will be a problem and the more energy you will have to live your life. When you are channeling your anger, you are really talking to your unconscious mind and asking it to do this chore for you and it will obey. You literally free up the energy that you were using to keep the anger under control and you also save the good energy that you would have used to do the chore otherwise. When you channel your anger on a regular basis which is many times a day, you will eventually not even have to say the words out loud in your head anymore. You will start to channel as a way of life, automatically and you will feel so much better.

You might want to give your anger a name so you can tell it to stand aside when it gets in the way and interferes with your life. Giving your anger a name, becoming intimate with it, will help you realize that your anger is your friend. The things that you are angry about are things that require your attention.

You can learn that expressing your anger when things happen to cause it, will not interfere with, but rather enhance your life. People get angry at other people and if you say to the people around you that you are angry, and tell them why in a nice way, they are more likely to respond in a manner that is much more helpful. If you keep it inside you may blow up at the people around you eventually or yell at them and strain the relationship. There is absolutely nothing wrong with saying, "I'm angry because..."

You may also deal with your anger by drawing it on paper or making a picture of doing something with it in your head or even saying out loud in a whisper, "I'm angry." This often provides relief when your anger is so large that it scares you. Your anger can feel nuclear at times and it then may feel unsafe to express. However, it is truly dangerous and destructive if you keep it under wraps. One of the benefits of a support group is that it offers a safe place to express your anger, get validated and at the same time learn new ways of dealing with it.

Finally, it is often helpful to write your anger down in your journal. Make a list (which you can add to) of all the things you are angry about, today and in the past. It may also be helpful to "weight" the items in the list. That is, give each item in the list a score from one to ten indicating how angry you are about that particular item. You may want to weight it from one to one hundred or one thousand, and some people actually use a scale of one to one million. Whatever feels right is what should be done.

Chapter 22:

Visualization Techniques

It's time to learn how to do visualizations. First you need to learn how to relax. Find a comfortable spot to lie down, perhaps on the sofa or the floor. Lie as flat as you can. Loosen your belt or pants if necessary so your clothing is not tight in any way. Place your hands by your sides. Out loud in your head, say, "Relax" in a calm, reassuring voice. (Repeat this often during the relaxation exercise.) Start to breathe slowly and deeply. Do the following slowly and deliberately. First, tighten the muscles in your left toes. Hold the tension for a few seconds then let the muscles relax. Next tighten the muscles in your left ankle. Hold a few seconds and let go. In a similar fashion, tighten and let go the muscles in your left calf, then your left thigh. Notice how relaxed your whole left leg feels. Repeat this for the right leg. Then tighten and release in order, your buttock muscles, pelvic muscles, tummy muscles and chest muscles. Then in order, make a fist with the left hand, tighten your left elbow, then make a muscle with the left arm. Repeat for the right arm. Now tighten your shoulder muscles, then your neck muscles, scalp muscles and finally your facial muscles. Notice how relaxed you feel. Again, say, "Relax" out loud in your head.

Now that you have done this for yourself, you might want to

tape your own voice giving the commands for the exercise. Your own voice will be soothing and will reinforce your ability to relax in response to hearing yourself speak the word "relax".

After doing this a few times, you will probably be able to reach a relaxed state by lying down and just saying, "Relax" out loud in your head. Don't try this while standing, you might relax so much that you will fall down! Now while you're still relaxed, try to picture a favorite vacation place, or place that you could be relaxed and safe by yourself. For example, a beach in the Caribbean, a mountain lake, the woods, anyplace that is safe and relaxing for you.

Imagine that you are actually in this safe place. You might smell ocean air or the scent of pine needles. You might see sea gulls or birds. You might hear the roar of the surf, the sound of the wind rustling the leaves in the trees or you might feel the sun on your body. Let yourself relax and be there in your safe place. Enjoy it. You can use this as a free vacation anytime you like. You can do this for a minute or two in your office during the afternoon for a refreshing break. No airfare, no waiting, an instant vacation anywhere in the world. Your imagination is your travel agent, and your visualizations are your vacation. When you are ready, let yourself float back to the "here and now." Relaxation exercises and visualizing your safe place facilitates the process of working with your inner child.

Start all your visualizations the same way. Close your eyes and say the word, "Relax" out loud in your head. Go to your safe place. Then do the individual visualization. In the beginning, your inner child may balk. She may not want to talk to you. Be patient with her, bearing in mind that she was a victim and has good reason not to trust you or anyone else until trust is established by the way you talk to her and treat her. Have empathy for her and what happened to her and she will know what's in your heart and start to trust you. When you get to know her and she trusts you, you will then be able to do the following inner child exercises.

Particularly for adoptees

1) Let yourself float back in time until you can see yourself around the age of seven. Walk into the picture and say hello to your younger self. Tell her you love her and ask her if she would like a hug. Ask her how she is feeling. Validate her feelings, but correct any mis-beliefs that she has about herself. Now ask her if she would like a hug from her natural mother. If she says no, ask her if she'll tell you why not.

> "The ability to [visualize] concentrate is a real propelling power of the totality of our psychic mechanism. Nothing elevates our capacity of action more than its development. Any success, no matter in which area, can be explained by the intelligent use of this capacity. No obstacle can permanently withstand the exceptional power of maximum concentration." – *What We May Be* - Pierro Ferrucci

If she says yes, visualize your natural mother hugging your younger self at age seven. Let the visualization continue as long as you wish, and when you are ready, slowly come back to the here and now.

2) Ask your seven-year-old self if she would like to move in with you. If she says yes, then in your mind, create an addition for her in your current home. She can have anything she wants. She can have dolphins to swim with, tame lions to play with, elephants to ride and any movie she wants to watch will instantly be on the television set. The idea is to get her away from the place where she might have experienced a great deal of pain. At some point during your visualizations you should explain to her that those pains and "bad" things from the past can never *never* happen again. Let her have fun in her childhood, stress free. She deserves it. At the end of the visualization, ask your inner child if it is all right for you to leave for a while, that you have some errands to do. Let her know that she can still play with the animals, toys etc. and that you'll be back soon. Tell her she

can always call you if she wants you to come back sooner. If she doesn't want you to go, you can suggest that she come with you. She can really fit into your pocket or ride on your shoulder. She might like that!

3) Imagine that you are in a large field, full of many different kinds of flowers. You might see birds and butterflies and grasshoppers, a beautiful blue sky and puffy clouds. Let yourself look around, see all of the flowers. You walk about in the field and come to a stream running through the middle of the field. There is an old creaky wooden bridge going across the stream to another field. Your adult self crosses over to the other side and you see your baby self, newborn, alone and crying. Go to her; talk to that young baby that you were, out loud in your head. Even though she is newborn, she can hear what you say, understand, and speak to you. Tell her she is lovable, that what happened wasn't her fault and hold her and let her cry for her mommy if she wants to. Ask her if she'd like to come across the stream with you and if she agrees, carry her across the bridge in your arms. Keep her with you and when you get a chance, draw a picture of you the adult and your young self sitting in the field and hugging. Write down what you felt during the visualization.

4) Visualize yourself being in a cocoon, peering out through the thin gauze, not seeing things as they really are, but fuzzy looking. Imagine that you, the adoptee, are going through a metamorphosis and becoming a butterfly. Becoming a butterfly is scary and painful, opening your wings for the first time, not knowing what you will be able to do. Imagine that you are unfolding your wings. You spread them and all of a sudden you are flying! Let yourself feel the sensation of floating, looking down at the world, exploring, going where you wish, feeling weightless and free. Recognize that as you do your work, face your demons, you will be like the butterfly,

unfolding your "wings," not knowing what you can do or be, but having the freedom to find out and finally be yourself.

"Inner child work is essential. It's the essence of growth as a whole person" - Cheryl Richardson

Chapter 23:

Affirmations

For adoptees

You need to intellectually know that nothing makes a baby unlovable. When you have that knowledge firmly implanted, you need to do and say the following: Imagine your younger self in your mind, picture that young child that you were and say **out loud** in your head, "It wasn't about you, although I know it feels like it. It wasn't about you and you are lovable and deserving. We are both okay." Look around you while you are saying this to prove to you and your inner child that you both are okay. You must absolutely believe, intellectually, that the above is true because you can never lie to your inner child.

"Traumatic events are extraordinary, not because they occur rarely, but rather because they overwhelm the ordinary human adaptations to life. Unlike commonplace misfortunes, traumatic events generally involve threats to [psychic] integrity... They confront human beings with the extremities of helplessness and terror and evoke the responses of catastrophe... The common denominator of psychological trauma is a feeling of intense fear, helplessness, loss of control and threat of annihilation." – *Trauma and Recovery*

I recommend that you repeat this affirmation out loud in your head *four times a waking hour* for the first month after you intellectually know that nothing makes a baby unlovable. If you do this faithfully, then by the end of the month the chances are excellent that you will feel much better about yourself.

You need to realize intellectually that what happened when you lost your mother can **never** happen again, though it can feel like it. It cannot happen because you are no longer the helpless child you were then. So, out loud in your head (while picturing that young child that you were) you can say, "I want you to know that *it* cannot happen again. I know it feels like it can, but I promise you it cannot and we're okay."

If you start to have an anxiety or panic attack or feel unsafe, you can say **out loud** in your head, "Nothing is happening now. I know it feels like it, but we're safe. RELAX." Don't forget to look around you while you say this to prove to both your inner child and yourself that nothing is indeed happening.

In general, an anxiety or panic attack occurs because something in today's world, perhaps something very subtle, reminds our unconscious mind of our original trauma (the loss of a mother) and it feels like it is about to happen again. Unfortunately, this is one of the common "legacies" of a trauma survivor.

For natural mothers

You need to intellectually know that you didn't stand a chance of keeping your baby in our society. **You must believe this!** To try and fight the money-making adoption machine is to lose. **You didn't have a chance!** When you have that knowledge firmly implanted, you need to do and say the following: Imagine your younger self in your mind, picture that young woman that you were when you were about to lose your baby and say **out loud** in your head, "It wasn't your fault, although I know it feels like it was. You had no choice and you are a lovable and deserving woman. We are both okay." Look around you while you are saying this to prove to you and your inner child that you both are okay. You must absolutely believe, intellectually, that the above is true because you can never lie to your inner child.

> "When a mother is forced to choose between the child and the culture, there is something abhorrently cruel and unconsidered about that culture. A culture that requires harm to one's soul in order to follow the culture's proscriptions is a very sick culture indeed." – *Women Who Run With the Wolves* – Clarissa Pinkola Estés

I recommend that you repeat this affirmation out loud in your head *four times a waking hour* for the first month after you intellectually know that you had no choice, It wasn't your fault. If you do this faithfully, then by the end of the month the chances are excellent that you will feel much better about yourself.

You need to realize intellectually that what happened when you lost your child can **never** happen again, though it can feel like it. It cannot happen because the child you surrendered is not a child anymore and the young resourceless woman you were then no longer exists. So, out loud in your head (picturing that young woman that you were) you can say, "I want you to know that *it* cannot happen again. I know it feels like it can, but I promise you it cannot and we're okay."

If you start to have a panic attack or feel unsafe, you can say **out loud** in your head, "Nothing is happening now. I know it feels like it, but we're safe. RELAX." Don't forget to look around you while you say this to prove to both your inner child and yourself that nothing is indeed happening.

In general, an anxiety or panic attack occurs because something in today's world, perhaps something very subtle, reminds your unconscious mind of the original trauma (the loss of a child) and it feels like it is about to happen again. Unfortunately, these attacks are one of the common "legacies" of a trauma survivor.

In general

Once you have been working with your inner child for a while, you will be able to create your own affirmations. Your inner child will always be able to tell you what she is afraid of and what she needs. You will then have the ability to decide (with her help of course) what to say to her on a regular basis to help her feel better.

Ultimately, the need to use affirmations will become less and less as you heal more an more, but you will always have the ability to help yourself in this way if necessary.

When we get street-lamped, our inner child is saying she "feels" rejected. The word "rejection" can cause an adoptee to have a melt-down. We need to remove that word from our vocabulary. Rejection is not a feeling, it's a thought that leads to terrifying feelings. If we don't think that word we will not feel those feelings. If an adoptee gets told "No" by her natural mother when she makes contact, she is not being rejected. Her mother is rejecting dealing with her own pain, anger and sadness. As long as the adoptee does not use the word rejected, she will not feel those terrifying emotions. Yes, being told "No" would be sad but without the word rejection floating around in your mind, being told "No" will be manageable.

Chapter 24:

Mourning for Adoptees

Probably the most painful part of an adoptee's healing is the mourning or grieving process. To heal, we must mourn our losses. Since most adoptees were not allowed to grieve the loss of their families, particularly their natural mother, their grief has been stuck in their bodies for 20, 30, 40 or more years and must be let out.

The adoptee has many things to mourn: The loss of her mommy, the loss of her natural mother, the loss of the relationship with her and the loss of all the milestones that would have been

> "Reliving a trauma may offer an opportunity for mastery, but most survivors do not consciously seek or welcome the opportunity. Rather they dread and fear it. Reliving a traumatic experience, whether in the form of intrusive memories, dreams or actions, carries with it the emotional intensity of the original event. The survivor is continually buffeted by terror and rage. These emotions are qualitatively different from ordinary fear and anger. They are outside the range of ordinary emotional experience, and they overwhelm the capacity to bear feelings." — *Trauma and Recovery*

shared with her. The loss of her natural mother's love has to be mourned and always, there is the loss of this unique connection to

if she is raised in the same religion, culture etc. as her birth family.

I believe that every adoptee needs to find a way to mourn all of these losses. A way to start would be to make a list (preferably in your journal) of all the things that were lost and "weight it" from 1 to 10 or 1 to 100 according to the level of sadness you feel. This exercise is a very effective technique. It will help you to identify your losses and assist in your grieving process.

In addition, to mourn your losses, you may chose to light a candle at home or in church, hold a "funeral" service for the things lost. Or just making a separate list of the things lost and bury the list in a box in a funeral type ritual. You might write a letter to your natural mother (preferably with your non-dominant hand, to allow your inner child to express herself) and read it aloud and then allow yourself to cry. You might visit your inner child and hold your inner child while the child cries for the loss of her mommy and all the other losses. There are a myriad of ways to mourn your losses and you can be creative. These are just a few examples of what you might do.

The adoptee deserves to have time to mourn the loss of her most sacred relationship and be treated as if there were a real death in her life today. You may want to take a few days or a week off to do your mourning. You need to let yourself cry and understand that every time you cry, you are healing. There is no non-painful way to do this work. And as you cry, you release harmful chemicals from your body in your tears and release healing chemicals within your blood stream. You will feel better when you let enough of the "poison" of your un-grieved losses out of your system.

If the adoptee is lucky enough to have a reunion and finds a mother who is willing to help her heal, they both could have tremendous healing by letting the adoptee be held in her natural mother's arms and cry out the pain she has been holding in all these years. Similarly, a natural mother needs to be able to grieve the loss

years. Similarly, a natural mother needs to be able to grieve the loss of her baby and it is important that she finds help in doing so.

Chapter 25:

One Woman's Journey

A letter from Tina, a 50-year-old adopted woman: "I first became aware of 'inner child' work while watching John Bradshaw on one of his 'Homecoming' television programs. While it seemed a bit weird, I thought I realized the possibilities of this stuff. It was only when I started using it in my therapy sessions and on my own that I was struck by the wonder and power of it.

"The beginning was difficult – resisting the temptation to have my adult mind speak for her, instead of just letting that little girl say what she had been wanting to say for so many years. And say it she does! She says things the adult me might not say; things I don't remember or the things I try to forget but she won't let me. Initially, visualization of 'her' was a problem, so I found a picture of my young self and concentrated on that. This may sound strange, but the next problem was freedom; accepting the fact that she could *do* anything she wanted, *say* anything she wanted, and *have* anything she wanted (including two ponies in my 18th floor apartment) – it was complete freedom. (You may ask why she has two ponies. She not only wanted a solid white one with wings – like the mythical

Pegasus, but one with spots – like the pinto that Tonto rode. Sounds reasonable to me!) At one point my therapist suggested that I treat her to something fun. Instantly I (or she?) thought of SEALS! I always loved pictures of seals as a child but there weren't any real ones around where I grew up in western North Carolina. So in my mind I took her to the Central Park Zoo where she fed and swam with the seals. She loves to do the same thing with the polar bears. That unlimited freedom allows her to stay under water with the seals and the bears as long as she wants. She doesn't have to come up for air.

"At first I visualized her in my adoptive parents' home, but my 'little girl' lives in my apartment with me now, where she feels safe. She watches all the people below from my apartment window, she goes to Central Park where she plays with other (inner) children and if she comes home before I do, Mother Goose is there to welcome her with a hug and her favorite food: a peanut butter and banana sandwich. The Mother Goose stuff came from a discussion I had with my therapist. When I was little, both my parents worked and very often, when I came home from school, I was alone in our big house. It always felt as though no one was ever going to come home again, and I was there, scared, and all alone. Then, in my inner child work, when she had gone through particularly painful memories, it was suggested that I reward her by telling her to go to the zoo to see the seals or bears. Then I added that she should go on home and I'll be there when I get off work. The first time I did this it seemed like a good idea, but the second time what I had told her gave me an uneasy feeling. The light went on! I was doing the same thing to her that had been done to me. Now she never goes home unless Mother Goose or I am there to greet her. I guess the biggest thing she's done, (so far), is (in my mind) to go to the circus where she could pet and ride any and all the animals she wanted, particularly the big cats. Even Bozo the Clown was waiting for her when she arrived holding up one of those signs with her name on it. She was there all day! All the circus people said hello to her and told her how happy they were that she was there. When I asked her about it, she was so excited that she jumped up and down and just couldn't stop talking.

"My inner child work takes the form of daily maintenance and emergency care. It was very easy in the beginning to forget to contact her and simply tell her I loved her. Only when she was stirred up did I talk to her. Knowing how hard it is for someone to break a habit, or erase that mental tape, I thought I should decide on a specific time, at least once a day, to talk to her, to tell her that she didn't have to worry about any responsibilities, that she was a sweet little girl, easy to love, that I loved her and to tell her that none of the bad stuff was happening now and would never happen again. I chose my morning Fifth Avenue bus ride to work. First, I do my inner child maintenance, then and only then I read whatever book I'm reading that week. Often, spending time with her is so enjoyable that I never get around to reading anything at all. The emergency care is done anytime she's feeling scared or sad, or anytime where she needs me to be there for her.

"The little child in me has the memories that were buried long ago – memories that bring up feelings never before expressed, or at least not listened to before. Allowing her to speak has made me realize the seriousness of what occurred in my young life and has made me want to help her feel that she is understood and loved. Being able to mentally go back to those times that were so painful and give 'her' the support and validation she never received was, and is, so healing. Inner child work has made me realize that she was a sweet little girl, not bad and not mean, and she deserved much more than the people around her were able to give. Inner child work has made me capable of loving her, and now, my adult self, the way she should have been loved from the beginning."

Chapter 26

The Respect We Never Got

I've looked into your eyes thousands of times and through them into your hearts and I've seen the *pain* and *anguish*. Alone you have had to endure what no human should ever have to endure. Alone, hiding from the world that exiled you. You who have lost your precious child. Your precious child who is Missing in Adoption and for whose loss you receive no respect. I know your pain for it is pain that we have shared together from the beginning. Exquisite pain because it is ours. At least we have that. Now, as to respect...

Without blaming anyone, I suggest we take a look at the respect we never got. To start with, we need to look at the beginning. The beginning was birth and separation for the mother and child. For the adoptive parents, the beginning was the discovery of being infertile or being unable to bring a child into the family any other way.

It was like a big plane crash in a field. All the mothers and babies lying there crying and the rescuers came and carried them off in different directions. When they got to the Emergency Room, they dusted them off, told them they were fine and sent them on their way. The mothers went home and the babies went to new homes. All were told they were fine. The most sacred relationship in the world has now gone up in smoke. They were told that there wasn't any accident, no crash, forget about it, just get on with your lives. The new parents of the babies were told the babies were fine and they should treat all the babies as if they were their own. As If. That's a great little phrase. As If.

As if is sort of like treating my cat as if she is the German Shepherd dog I really wanted. But I get so frustrated. She won't fetch, she doesn't bark at the door and she won't get my slippers. I love her, but I get so angry she doesn't behave the way I want her to. As if just doesn't work.

So what really happened to each of those mothers and babies from the plane crash? As I see it, there is no substantial difference between the experience of losing a child to death and losing a child to adoption except if there were a real death of a child shortly after birth, the mother's family and friends would have gathered around and said to her I am so sorry your baby died. You must be sad, let me comfort you, I know you hurt, let me ease your pain. I know you must be angry, let me help you. There would be a funeral and grieving and acknowledgment of what really happened, and there would be a grave to go to and there would be validation and healing. This mother would be given respect.

Instead, the mother who loses her child to adoption experiences the psychological death of her child. Instead of comfort, she gets told she did a brave and noble, unselfish, loving thing and she must forget about it, go on with her life. No one wants to help her talk about it, acknowledge it, cry about it, or mourn the loss of her child. So the loss becomes almost unresolvable. The grief stays stuck in her body and keeping pain in is destructive. She has to go into a kind of shock to survive, hit the pause button on her life and she goes numb. Life is forever changed. You can't really live that way, but you can exist. She gets no respect.

If there were a real death of a mother shortly after birth, at some point, the child's father would tell the child that mommy died and it is so sad that this happened to you and you must hurt, let me comfort you and ease your pain and I know you must be angry, let me help you... and there would be pictures and stories and a grave to visit, and grieving, and eventually the child would find out that mommy didn't die on purpose. This child would be given respect.

Instead for the child whose mother surrenders her to adoption, the child suffers the psychological death of her mother. But she is told that she is special and chosen and lucky. She is supposed to forget that there was another mother. Make believe this is your only family, make believe that all is well. "As if" it is your own. The message is that it is a good thing your mother is not there for you, is dead for you. You are not allowed to be sad about it, acknowledge the pain, anger or sadness, perhaps even to yourself. You are not allowed to mourn the loss of your own mother. The grief gets stuck in your body and keeping in pain is destructive. (So is keeping in anger and sadness). The child has to go into a kind of shock and go numb. You can't really live that way, but you can pretend. We adoptees are great pretenders. This child gets no respect.

What would happen if your mother died today and you were told you couldn't cry, you couldn't go to the funeral and you had to make believe she never existed. What would happen to you? Take a moment and think about it.

Isn't that what happened to most people in adoption in some way?

It occurs to me that if we really had respect for the mother and the child we would do all we could to preserve the sanctity of that relationship and not separate them at all. If the mother and child could not possibly stay together, then giving her respect when she lost her child, the mother's family and friends would have gathered around and said to her, "I am so sorry you couldn't keep your baby. You must be sad, let me comfort you. I know you hurt, let me ease your pain. I know you must be angry, let me help you." Then there would be grieving and acknowledgment of what really happened.

If the mother and child could not possibly stay together, then giving the adoptee respect when she lost her mother, the new family would say, "You must be sad you lost your natural family, it's okay to cry about it. I'm sad too, you must hurt. Let me comfort you, you must be angry, let me help you, be with you and hold you."

If adoptive parents got respect, they would have gotten complete information on their adopted child and the truth about the effects on their child of losing the natural family. The adoption agency and others would have acknowledged the sadness of infertility or inability to have a child on one's own. Their pain and anger would have been acknowledged and they would have been encouraged to grieve the child they couldn't have on their own.

Ignoring the realities of adoption increases the pain and hurt. How can anyone function well if they're told that what is true isn't and what isn't true is?

For example, what if I lose my leg in an accident right after birth? And they tell me I didn't lose my leg right after I was born, I was mistaken. But it hurts, mommy, and yet it still feels like something is missing. And I keep stumbling around as if I had only one leg (they wouldn't lie about that would they?) and I don't know why I'm having trouble managing as a two-legged person...

Our society doesn't want to acknowledge what has happened to all of us, to give us respect. Truth be told, I lost more than a leg, I lost my mother. Wait, I've got a prosthesis, a new mother, a substitute. Why doesn't it work just as well? Why does it still hurt? Of course our natural mothers lost a baby... but they got no replacement, no substitute.

Respect is truth, no secrets, absolute honesty. We can all deal with the truth.

Have we in adoption had our eyes wide shut? Isn't it time they were wide open?

Well, how can we give ourselves the respect we never got? By learning to experience our feelings. By learning to make "I" statements about our experience.

By learning to say I feel sad because_____, I feel angry because_____, I hurt because_____ (fill in the blank). When we say these things out loud for the first time and get validated for the first time, our feelings become real in a way they can never be if unexpressed. Once our feelings become real, we can start to understand why we feel what we feel and once we understand why we feel what we feel, we can start to change the way our experience affects us today.

We can respect ourselves by expressing our anger at what happened to us. Having anger about something that happened to us and expressing it does not make us angry people. We need to express it. If we don't talk our anger out, we will surely act it out or act it in, in either case, it is destructive. It is poison and will poison our lives and relationships unless we release it.

We can respect ourselves by expressing our sadness. Feeling sad about something sad that happened does not make us cry babies or wimps. We need to express it. Keeping our pain in is destructive. It is poison and it will poison our lives and our relationships unless we release it.

The only way that I know of to be truly happy is to give ourselves the respect of feeling all of our feelings. If we don't feel the bad ones, we cannot feel the good ones.

Those around us often try to minimize our losses, our experience. We must not buy into that. We can respect ourselves by acknowledging the true extent of the effects on us of the events at the beginning. If we don't acknowledge the full extent of our wounds, we cannot heal. Only by acknowledging the truth can we begin to heal from our wounds. If I am in an accident and go to the ER and they don't examine my wounds, don't clean the depths of my wounds and get the dirt or poison out, I will get an infection, the wound may heal superficially, but the infection is there nevertheless and I will pay a price. Only when I respect myself and take the risk of opening that wound again and clean it out will I be able to truly heal.

Healing involves a lot of pain, but the alternative... I guess we have all lived it. We need to give ourselves the respect to climb the mountain of pain that leads to healing. The mountain is steep, but climbable. There are many crevices on the way up, but each crevice still puts you closer to the top. We are all here in this adoptive family to help each other, nurture each other, support each other, share with each other and learn from each other on this road to respect and healing.

Clarissa Pinkola Estés, who wrote *Women Who Run with the Wolves*, has said that those who have been "abandoned" and face it and work it through can become the strongest people on the face of the earth.

Don't doubt it for a second. Only the truly brave do this work, come to conferences and support groups and work it through.

The alternative to doing the work — Well, we can continue to bury our heads like an ostrich, but if we do, we will likely get kicked in the behind and not see it coming. Or to put it another way, if we continue to swim in Denial we will likely get bitten by a crocodile.

"Adoption Loss is the only trauma in the world where the victims are expected by the whole of society to be grateful" - The Reverend Keith C. Griffith, MBE

"One of the saddest things of all is that so many adoptees and moms are afraid to take the risk of healing which is necessary to pursue one's dreams"

"The prisoner disintegrated because he could never find out what he was guilty of" - The Trial by Kafka

"People cannot endure inexplicable worthlessness" - John D. MacDonald

`Not to have knowledge of what happened before you were born is to be condemned to live forever as a child.' - Cicero (c. 106-43 BC)

Part Six:

Appendices

Appendix A:

What Adoptees
Do Not Wish to Hear

1. You're special because you're adopted.
2. You were chosen.
3. Your natural mother loved you so much that she gave you up.
4. You're lucky.
5. It doesn't matter.
6. You shouldn't be angry.
7. You shouldn't be sad.
8. You should be careful what you ask for – you might get it.
9. By finding her, you're invading her life.
10. Why are you interested in someone who didn't want you?
11. Why do you want to find someone you didn't ever know?
12. Ever since you started searching you have become obsessed.
13. But your adoptive parents love(d) you so much...
14. But you're hurting your adoptive parents...
15. Babies don't remember anything.
16. You're being ungrateful!
17. You have no respect for your adoptive parents.
18. Get over it!
19. If she loved you, she wouldn't have given you away.

20.   You're being over sensitive.
21.   Forget it and get on with your life.
22.   Why would you want to find her?
23.   It's the past; you can't change it.
24.   You have no right to disturb her life.
25.   But your adoptive parents really wanted you...
26.   What's wrong? Weren't your adoptive parents good enough?
27.   You're being selfish and disrespectful!
28.   Didn't your parents do a good enough job?
29.   How many mothers do you need?
30.   Oh...you're one of them?
31.   You adopted children should respect her privacy.
32.   But you look like you come from such a good family...
33.   But you don't look adopted...
34.   Well, maybe that's the way it was meant to be.
35.   If she didn't want you then, why would she want you now?
36.   You might be opening Pandora's box .

You can add your own things not to say here!

Appendix B:

What Natural Parents
Do Not Wish to Hear

1. Forget about it (your baby) and get on with your life.
2. Leave well enough alone; she has another family now.
3. You did the right thing.
4. You will destroy/disrupt her/his life if you make contact.
5. You would have been unable to provide for your child.
6. It was better for the baby to have two parents.
7. Let sleeping dogs lie.
8. Your child has her own family now.
9. But you've had other children and you should be happy now.
10. Why don't you just let it go?
11. Your child was better off.
12. It's water under the bridge now.
13. If she needs you, she'll come searching for you. You shouldn't search for her!
14. You made the decision and you can't change your mind.
15. But you're not *really* her/his mother.
16. That was a long time ago. What's the matter with you?
17. S/he's turned out to be a nice person, so you should be grateful.
18. S/he's in a good home.

19.   You have other children.
20.   Concentrate on your immediate family.
21.   You have to let her go.
22.   She's not yours.
23.   Think of her real parents.
24.   Don't be selfish.
25.   She has a mother.
26.   You would not have been a good mother.
27.   Respect "their" privacy.
28.   One day you'll forget her.
29.   You need help!
30.   When are you going to get over this?
31.   Be glad you did not have an abortion.
32.   How many other kids do you have?
33.   She looks like her adoptive parents.
34.   She will never forgive you.
35.   So what else is going on?
36.   Don't tell your other kids.
37.   You've really become obsessed with this.
38.   One day you'll throw that picture away.
39.   Why now, after all these years?
40.   You lost your rights a long time ago.
41.   I am grateful that you gave me up.

You can add your own things not to say here!

Appendix C:

What Adoptive Parents Do Not Wish to Hear

1. How much did she/he cost?
2. Why did you adopt – couldn't you have your "own" child?
3. Did you buy that baby?
4. Maybe now that you adopted, you'll have "your own" child.
5. She looks nothing like either of you.
6. What are you going to do when she looks for her natural parent?
7. Do you know her "real" parents?
8. I sure hope she fits into your family!
9. Why didn't her real mom want her?
10. Don't even tell her she is adopted, she'll never know.
11. Too bad you had to adopt!
12. Whose fault is it you can't get pregnant?
13. What is she?
14. Couldn't you afford a white child?
15. What will you do when she starts looking?
16. Whose eyes does she have?
17. What religion are her parents?
18. Is her father black?

You can add your own things not to say here!

Appendix D:

About Sealed Adoption Records

As of the writing of this book, five states in the United States, Alaska, Delaware, Hawaii, Kansas and Tennessee allow adoptees access to their original birth certificates. In November 1998, the citizens of Oregon, voted in referendum to give adoptees access to their original birth certificates, but the law is being challenged by those who claim that adoptees have no right to such information because they might upset their mothers. Ohio gives adoptees access to their original birth certificates if they were born before 1963. Various other states will conduct a search on the adoptee's behalf, but if her mother says no contact, the adoptee can still conduct a search on her own.

Most people who search, whether born in a state which allows access to records or not, will succeed if they are tenacious. However, why should they have to spend so much time and money and energy and emotion to find out their past?

In most countries outside of the North American continent, adoptees have access to their records when they reach the age of majority. In Holland they recently lowered the age from 14 to 12 for adoptees to get their original birth certificate because they know the importance of having that knowledge during adolescence. In Belgium, Holland, Sweden, Australia and New Zealand the governments have gone to great lengths to stop the separation of mother and child because they know that the separation devastates the lives of both.

When the adoption records were opened in England in 1976 (Child Welfare Act of 1975) the rationale was that an adopted person's right to their origins superceded anyone's "supposed" right to privacy. Additionally, the social workers and others who spearheaded the drive to give adoptees access to their records stated that they had been asking the wrong question. "We've been asking ourselves why those adopted people wanted to search. The real question is what have we done as a society to make adopted people afraid to search?"

Privacy issues have been touted as arguments against access to records by those few individuals who oppose an adopted person's or natural parent's access to the information on their lost relative. In fact, in most states in the United States, the adoption records were sealed to protect the parties involved from blackmail from the outside world, not to prevent contact with each other. Moreover, in most relinquishment papers in the US, the new mother is surrendering her right to parent her child, nothing more. Contrary to the statements by those against access to records, there is no mention of privacy or searching or caring in the surrender documents. In addition, since most state laws have the proviso that a judge can, if she deems there to be good cause, give the adopted person all of her information, there is no guarantee of privacy in the first place.

"The law must be consonant with life. It cannot and should not ignore broad historical currents of history. Mankind is possessed of no greater urge than to try to understand the age-old questions: 'Who am I?' and 'Why am I?' Even now, the sands and ashes of the continents are being sifted to find where we made our first steps as man. Religions of mankind often include ancestor worship in one way or another. For many the future is blind without sight of the past. Those emotions and anxieties that generate our thirst to know

the past are not superficial and whimsical. They are real and they are 'good cause' under the law of man and God."
– the Hon. Wade Weatherford, S. Carolina Circuit Court Judge.

New York Newsday, LETTERS, December 1990

Past the Age of Consent by Joe Soll

If I as an adult want to get married, do I need my parents permission? Do I need their permission to get a divorce? Why, then, does Ann Landers in her advice column of Dec 12 tell the "Interim Parent" from Salem, Ore. that she thinks adopted children should get permission from their adoptive parents to have a reunion with their birth families? And why is an adult who was adopted as a child referred to as an "adopted child"?

As a psychotherapist, and an adoptee and a supposedly free human being, I take issue with having to ask permission from my parents to do anything. That's infantalizing and demeaning.

I have helped literally thousands of adoptees and natural parents reunite — without the adoptive parents' permission — and not once in eight years have I seen an adopted person rejected by his or her natural parents; most adoptees get closer to their adoptive parents after the reunion.

Adoptees did not ask to be surrendered to adoption. They should certainly have the right of every other human being on this planet to know who brought them into this world and know their heritage. They have the right to be equal and not eternally thought of as children. Adults negotiate their relationships without having to ask permission from anyone.

Appendix E:

Loss in The Adoption Hand-Off
(by Darlene Gerow and inspired by Ken Watson, Ph.D.)

Before we begin, please list your most favorite in each of the five categories.

Write your choices down.

Your most favorite: **Sound**

Your most favorite: **Taste**

Your most favorite: **Smell**

Your most favorite: **Place**

Your most favorite: **Person**

Although difficult, choose among your favorites, discarding the one you will miss least. Continue discarding until all of your favorites are gone.

Take careful note of how it feels to imagine losing all of your most favorites, including your most favorite person

A child's favorites are perhaps easier to recognize, but please consider the favorites of babies and the very real losses they experience during the hand-off at adoption.

Baby's most favorite **Sound**	The regular in and out of my mother's breathing and the dependable rhythm of her heart beat. But mostly the sound of her voice.
Baby's most favorite **Taste**	My mother's milk, created exclusively for me. And the taste of her skin, her breast. It is all one.
Baby's most favorite **Smell**	The scent of my mother's skin as I bury my face in her neck. It is basic and right. It is where I belong.
Baby's most favorite **Place**	Cradled in my mother's arms, next to the sounds and smells and tastes that I have experienced since my conception. This is my home.
Baby's most favorite **Person**	My mother is my universe. She is a part of me, just as I am a part of her. No one can replace her. If I am separated from her, I will long for her my entire life.

Adoptees, regardless of their age, whether they are newborn or older, domestically adopted or foreign, give up all of their favorite things when they are adopted.

The loss begins with their name. They lose all information about themselves and their origins. They lose their identity.

They lose it all. They lose the smells and tastes and sounds and places and people with whom they are familiar... all of their favorites. Everything they have ever known is gone and changed forever.

Their greatest loss, which you surely understand, is the loss of their favorite person. Mommy! They lose their most favorite person irrevocably.

If there must be a separation of mother and child, if there is no other way, by recognizing an adoptee's loss, we can endeavor to ease the pain by maintaining as much of her previous life as possible. With empathy we can make their transition more humane.

Author's comments:

There is some evidence that a newborn "knows" when she is looking into the eyes of her natural mother or someone else. This may explain the apparent high percentage of vision problems among the adopted population. If the infant does indeed know when she is not looking into her natural mother's eyes, she has lost another of her favorite thing and her general anxiety would be even more pronounced.

"The bond between a mother and her child is naturally sacred. It is physical, psychological and spiritual. It is very resilient and very flexible. It can stretch very far - naturally. Any artificial or violent injury to this "stretch" constitutes a serious psychic trauma to both mother and child - for all eternity. This means that children need their mothers and mothers need their children - whether or not a mother is married or unmarried." - *Mothers On Trial, The Battle For Children and Custody* - by Phyllis Chesler

A mother's losses from the Adoption Hand-off are the flip side of the adoptee's losses. Just as big, just as important, just as irrevocable, just as painful, just as sad and just as tragic.

Appendix F:

Things to Do with Your Inner Child

Here is a list of some fun things for you and your Inner Child to do together:

1) Do something you've always wanted to do as a child, but were never allowed to do, *e.g.,* let the dog sleep in your bed with your inner child EVERY night.

2) Swim with the dolphins – for some it would be specifically be Flipper!

3) Swim with the polar bears (they won't hurt you and you don't have to come up for air.)

4) Go to the zoo/circus and get to go "backstage."

5) Own a pony (or two.)

6) Own a hawk or an eagle.

7) Have any toy(s) in the world that you want.

8) When you, the adult, can't be home with your inner child, let Mama Bear or Mother Goose or Mickey Mouse take care of her.

9) If you don't have an extra room for your inner child, then build one in your mind – even if it's on the 30th floor and sticking out from your building.

10) Fly.

11) Sit on a cloud.

12) Let her go to a public park alone and know she won't have to worry about getting hurt by anyone.

13) Have a tub as big as a swimming pool.

14) If she has had a particularly scary day, tell her there are two friendly (only to her) giants outside the door to protect her.

15) Let her stay up as late as she wants.

16) She is no longer allergic and can have a cat, dog, iguana, cockatoo, or whatever animals she wants as pets. (Tell her out loud in your head that she doesn't have to be allergic anymore.)

17) Take her to a museum and let her pick up or touch anything she wants.

18) (Particularly pre-reunion) Visualize your inner child and let her natural mother walk into the picture and give her a hug.

Here are some Healing Rituals for you and your Inner Child to do together:

Light a candle and then:

1) Let the flame represent the burning desire to have something that doesn't exist anymore, like wanting to go back and this time be raised by your natural mother. When you are ready to stop wanting something that is impossible to happen, blow out the flame that holds you back from living your life, that burns you with a desire for the impossible.

2) Let the flame represent your losses. It's time to mourn what you didn't have. Let the candle be a memorial, a symbol of what you lost so you can grieve, cry for all that you have tried to repress for all of these years.

3) Let the flame be the spark that you have that has carried you to this point in your healing process. Cherish the flame. Acknowledge your strength.

4) Let the flame be your energy to dig a hole in your back yard or the woods and bury some of your unattainable desires. (You might actually write them down on paper and bury them in a box or can etc.)

Appendix G:

From the News

BENEFITS OF BREAST FEEDING by Liz Grapentine

Breast-feeding also nourishes a baby's heart and soul. Snuggled warm in mother's arms, hearing the heartbeat she heard in the womb for 9 months, drinking in her mother's warm, sweet milk, baby is drinking in her mother's love, as well. Breast-feeding, of physical necessity, involves intimate physical and emotional bonding between mother and baby. Baby is held at just the right distance from mother's face to be able to really see her, and only her. Because breast-milk digests so quickly (every 1.5–3 hours), baby is held most of the time. When a mother must devote that much time to her baby, it certainly enhances the probability that she and her baby will truly emotionally connect with one another. Mother will be with baby enough to get acquainted with her baby's needs, and know how best to respond to them. When a baby's mother is able to do this, her baby will learn to trust her mother, thus forming a healthy base for her relationships with all others she will encounter throughout her lifetime. A breast-fed baby knows that her needs will be met with love and concern, that she is valuable enough to come first to others who love her, and that she can trust others in the future to meet her needs, and she theirs. A breast-fed baby knows how to find home.

At the same time, the breast-feeding relationship nourishes the mother, as well. She learns to mother by looking to the needs of her child, initially while breast-feeding. Then, she can apply that model of need parenting to the rest of her mothering experiences. In a very real sense, baby is growing the very mother she needs in this process. This kind of child-led mothering – mothering through following the needs of the individual child – is often called attachment parenting.

There are other benefits that accrue to the breast-feeding mother. Women who have breast-fed their babies have lower rates of breast, uterine, endometrial and ovarian cancers. Breast-feeding mothers reduce their chances of osteoporosis. And they lose weight more quickly in the early post-partum months. The breast-feeding mother is empowered by her decision to breast-feed, as she realizes that she alone is capable of providing the best food for her baby.

The Associated Press, December 2, 1997

Moms Urged to Nurse for Full-Year

CHICAGO (AP) – Mothers should breast-feed their babies for at least a year, according to a pediatric group's recommendation that replaces a 15-year-old statement suggesting six to 12 months of nursing. Feedings should begin within an hour of birth and continue eight to 12 times every 24 hours, with each feeding lasting 20 to 30 minutes, the American Academy of Pediatrics said Monday. And breast-feeding should continue past the child's first birthday "for as long as mutually desired," said the nation's largest group of children's doctors.

Almost all babies, including those born sick or prematurely, should be breast-fed, according to the new recommendation. The only exceptions should be for mothers who use illegal drugs or have tuberculosis or the AIDS virus, the academy said. Critics said the new recommendations and the huge commitment they require – up to six hours a day – may be out of touch with reality.

"I think these guidelines will present a problem for new mothers who have no choice but to go back into the work force quickly," said Janice Rocco of the National Organization for Women. "They might already feel guilty about working, and this might add even more to that." Companies can help by providing private rooms where nursing mothers can pump their breasts so their milk can be bottled, refrigerated and fed to their babies later, said the academy, based in the Chicago area.   Research has shown that breast-fed babies are less likely to get such ailments as diarrhea, ear infections and bacterial meningitis than babies who are fed infant formula. Some studies suggest nursing also may protect against such diseases as diabetes, lymphoma and allergies.

Also, mothers who breast-feed reduce their risk of ovarian and pre-menopausal breast cancer, and they return to their pre-pregnancy weight more quickly than mothers who use bottles, studies show.

Los Angeles Times News Service

A Mother's Love, Brain Linked by Robert Lee Holz

Deprivation called harmful to growth

NEW ORLEANS – Exploring the biology of mother love, researchers reported that parental care makes such a lasting impression on an infant that maternal separation or neglect can profoundly affect the brain's biochemistry, with lifelong consequences for growth and mental ability.

Children raised without being regularly hugged, caressed, or stroked – deprived of the physical reassurance of normal family attention – have abnormally high levels of stress hormones, according to new research on Roumanian orphans raised in state-run wards.   Moreover, new animal research reveals that without the attention of a loving care-giver early in life, some of an infant's brain cell's simply commit suicide. While the growing brain naturally prunes cells during development – losing up to half by adulthood – the neurons in the neglected animals died at twice the rate as those animals kept with their mothers.

"What we found shocked us," psychologist Mark Smith at the Du Pont Merck Research Labs in Wilmington, Del., said Monday. Smith analyzed the effects of maternal deprivation in laboratory animals. "Maternal separation caused these cells in the brain to die. The effects of maternal deprivation may be much more profound than we had imagined," she said. "Does this have implications for humans? Frankly, I hope not, but I suspect there may be."

Scientists have known for decades that maternal deprivation can mark children for life with serious behavioral problems, leaving them withdrawn, apathetic, slow to learn, and prone to chronic illness. But a range of new research, presented in New Orleans at a meeting of the Society for Neuroscience, reveals for the first time the biochemical consequences of emotional neglect on the developing brain.

"It has been known for a long time that early experience is able to shape the brain and behavior," said Ron de Kloet, an expert on stress and the endocrine system at the University of Leiden in the Netherlands. "Only recently have we been able to go into the brain and measure what is actually happening in early experience." It is the relationship between parental care, the neurobiology of touch, and the chemistry of stress that lies at the heart of the new insights in how a newborn brain takes shape. Researchers said that neglect can warp the brain's developing neural circuits so that they produce too much or too little of the hormones that control responses to stress, causing permanent changes in the way an organism behaves and responds to the world around it. In infants, high levels of stress can impair growth and development of the brain and body.

In animal studies, ""the presence of the mother ensures these stress hormones remain at a nice low level," said Michael Meaney at the Douglas Hospital Research Center in Montreal. New laboratory research by Meaney and other neuroscientists highlights the long-range biochemical consequences of neglect and the effect of maternal care on the development of brain regions that control responses to stress.

Studies with laboratory animals show that the simple act of a mother licking her pup triggers a surprisingly subtle chain of biochemical events inside the infant's brain.   As the mother physically comforts her newborn, it stimulates the production of key biochemicals that inhibit production of a master stress hormone called CRH. To determine whether these new laboratory insights apply to human child rearing, researchers are now assessing the changing brain chemistry of children and the attention then receive from their primary care giver, be it mother, father, or day-care worker.

Rockland County Journal News
September 10, 1996

Remnants of babies stay with mothers for years
By Karl Leif

Mothers and children have a special bond, and it is deeper than you might imagine. It turns out a mother carries in her bloodstream, for decades after they are born, a little piece of every baby she has had.

A research team that includes a Wayne State University (Detroit) professor stumbled across the discovery while trying to develop a noninvasive test for detecting birth defects. The finding raises a host of interesting questions, not the least of which is how the obviously alien cells manage to eke out a living for decades without attracting attention from the mother's immune system.

"Everybody's curious about this," said Dr. Mark Evans, a medical professor and member of the team. But the goal of the study is to develop a reliable test for birth defects, a task that may take several more years. As part of its research, the team drew the blood of pregnant women and screened the blood for fetal cells. In the blood samples from women who ended up having female children they found Y chromosomes, the genetic marker of a male baby. "We knew that didn't belong to the mom, and it didn't seem to belong to the current fetus," said Dr. Diana W. Bianchi, chief of perinatal genetics at Boston's New England Medical Center.

Thinking it could be a lab mistake, the researchers looked again, this time drawing blood from women who previously had carried boys but who now were pregnant with girls. All four women carried fetal cells with Y chromosomes. Then they looked at eight mothers who were not pregnant but who had given birth to a son in the past three decades. Six of the eight carried fetal cells with a Y chromosome. One of the women had delivered her last boy 27 years ago.

"As a working mother who travels quite a bit it's comforting to me to know that I carry my children with me," Bianchi said with a laugh. The cells they found are immature white blood cells of the male babies, though Bianchi is sure the cells of female babies also are left behind. "It's just much easier to track the Y chromosomes," she said. Female cells occur in very small numbers in the mother's bloodstream and must be sorted with several techniques to be isolated for study.

"It's literally like looking for needle in a haystack," Evans said. If the proposed blood test for fetal genetic defects can be perfected, the technique would be safer than amniocentesis which involves piercing the uterus with a large needle. Amniocentesis can cause miscarriages about once in every 200 tests. "If we can get this to work, you could get the same answers that we get with an invasive test," Evans said.

The New York Times Science Watch
APRIL 30, 1991

The Key Role of Smell in an Infant's Bonding

For a newborn infant, whose fuzzy vision registers only the most obtuse rendering of its mother it is not love at first sight but love at first scent. Furthermore as documented in the April Issue of Pediatrics, overzealous application of perfume during the first few days after birth can mislead the baby and block bonding.

"Newborns learn to prefer the odor of their mother and this preference allows them to maintain contact and to find the mother's nipple for the purpose of nursing," said Dr. Michael Leon, professor of psychology at the University of California at Irvine. "A new mother wearing very heavy perfume may overwhelm her actual odor and make it difficult for natural bonding to occur."

Research on rats and other mammals had revealed similar patterns. Dr. Leon and his colleagues discovered that the "primary olfactory memory" is established in as little as 10 minutes for humans. However there must be supplemental tactile stimulation or this special memory will not become permanently enmeshed in the brain's processes.   This insures that infants do not attach themselves to other airborne odors. "We took babies, with their mothers' permission and placed them in a bassinet where they were exposed to a citrus odor while we stroked them lightly on the torso for 10 minutes," said Dr. Leon. "The next day they were again placed in a bassinet and allowed to turn toward the citrus odor."

"Almost invariably they expressed a preference by turning toward that odor." Besides helping relieve nursing deficiencies these experiments could "expedite the diagnosis" and early treatment of cognitive disorders in newborns, the researchers wrote.

The New York Times Editorials
AUGUST 11, 1993

Impact of Separation by Joe Soll

To the Editor:

I am concerned about the lack of knowledge about the effects of separation of mother and child immediately after birth ("Cutting the Baby in Half." editorial Aug. 1.) Your statement that a child will suffer injury if separated from its psychological – as opposed to biological – family is not entirely accurate.

What we now know about the separation of the neonate from its mother indicates a lifelong impact on both mother and child. The neonate has already bonded with its mother. In the last trimester the fetus knows the sounds and rhythms of its mother's heartbeat and respiration, knows mother's voice and immediately after birth "memorizes" her smell.

The separation from everything safe is a psychic shock to the neonate, a trauma that leads to enduring psychological issues, including identity and relationship problems and low self-esteem. (Incubator babies exhibit some of the same effects later in life.) Mothers who have surrendered children will have similar difficulties.

We should follow the Australian example: A mother may not surrender a child to adoption until it is two months old; after surrender, the mother has two months to change her mind, and if she does so, the child is immediately returned to her. In addition, pregnant women need to be given nonjudgmental counseling about the ramifications of their choices. The psychological needs of babies must be understood so that decisions are truly in the child's best interest.

Appendix H:

Resources and Readings

Adoption Crossroads is affiliated with 470+ search/support groups, referrals to therapists, attorneys in eight countries and resources for search help worldwide. For information, call Adoption Crossroads at 845-268-0283 or 212-988-0110. Write to: 74 Lakewood Drive, Congers, New York, NY 10920. Visit the Adoption Crossroads web site at: www.AdoptionCrossroads.org which has over 40 pages of information on search and support. Email Adoption Crossroads at: info@adoptioncrossroads.org

Joe Soll facilitates healing weekends six times annually. For the healing weekend schedule, location and travel information, visit www.AdoptionCrossroads.org/healing.shtml.

Adoption Crossroads is a charitable, 501 c (3), not-for-profit corporation chartered in New York State. Adoption Crossroads is a member of the Human Services Council of NY City and the Yorkville Civic Council. Adoption Crossroads is also an affiliate of the International Soundex Reunion Registry and the co-organizer the NY State Task Force on Adoption.

Recommended Readings:

Adoption Related:

Allen, Elizabeth Cooper, *Mother, Can You Hear Me?*

Andersen, Robert, *2ⁿᵈ Choice: Growing Up Adopted*
_____, & Tucker, Rhonda, *The Bridge Less Traveled*

* Gravelle, K., & Fischer S., *Where Are My Birthparents? A Guide for Teenage Adoptees.*

Guttman, Jane, *The Gift Wrapped in Sorrow*

Hughes, Ann H., *Soul Connection : A Birthmother's Healing Journey*

Lifton, Betty Jean, *Journey of the Adopted Self*
_____, *Lost and Found*
_____, *To Prison With Love*

Musser, Sandra, *I Would Have Searched Forever*
* _____, *To Prison With Love*

Pavao, Joyce Maguire, *The Family of Adoption*

Robinson, Evelyn, *Adoption and Loss: the hidden grief*

Schaefer, Carol, *The Other Mother*

Solinger, Rickie, *Wake Up Little Susie: Single Pregnancy & Race Before Roe v. Wade,*

Soll, Joe & Buterbaugh, Karen W. *Adoption Healing... a path to recovery for mothers who lost children to adoption*

Sorosky, A., Baran, A. & Pannor, R. *The Adoption Triangle. Sealed or Open Records: How They Affect Adoptees, Birthparents and Adoptive Parents*

Taylor, Pat, *Shadow Train: A Journey Between Relinquishment and Reunion*

Verrier, Nancy Newton, *The Primal Wound: Legacy of the Adopted Child*

Inner Child:

Asper, Kathryn, *Abandoned Child Within: On Losing and Regaining Self-Worth*

Bradshaw, John, *Homecoming. Reclaiming and Championing Your Inner Child*

Ferrucci, Piero, *What We May Be: Techniques for Psychological and Spiritual Growth Through Psychosynthesis*

Miller, Alice, *Drama of The Gifted Child: The Search for the True Self*

Stettbacher, J. Konrad, *Making Sense Out of Suffering*

Whitfield, Charles L., *Healing the Child Within*

General:

Bass, Ellen & Davis, Laura, *The Courage to Heal: Guide for Women Survivors of Sexual Abuse*

Chamberlain, David, *Babies Remember Birth*

Chodorow, Nancy J., *The Reproduction of Mothering*

Edelman, Hope, *Motherless Daughters: The Legacy of Loss*

Estés, Clarissa Pinkola, *Women Who Run With The Wolves, The Gift of Story* and *the Faithful Gardner*

Gallagher, Winifred, *I.D.: How Heredity and Experience Make You Who You Are*

Hermann, Judith, *Trauma and Recovery*

Neubauer, Peter B. et al., *Nature's Thumbprint: The New Genetics of Personality*

Pearce, Joseph Chilton, *Magical Child*

Sark, *Living Juicy: Daily Morsels for your Creative Soul*

Verny, Thomas, *Secret Life of the Unborn Child*

* (May be ordered from Adoption Crossroads.) All others may be ordered on-line at http://www.adoptioncrossroads.org. Click on Book Store. Email:joesoll@adoptioncrossroads.org

Epilogue

"..I'm... looking for something, something
sacred I lost... I'm searching for something,
Taken out of my soul, something I'd never
lose, something somebody stole... in the
middle of the night!..." – *River of Dreams* –
Billy Joel

My voice teacher told me a story about one of the most
famous of all composers whose son used to go to the piano and play
"Do Re Mi Fa Sol La Ti " and walk away. His father felt compelled
to go to the piano and hit the "Do" key to finish the sequence.

As adoptees and natural mothers, our natural sequence is
not finished and we feel a deep seated (the deepest) need to
complete it. Truly compelling beyond the comprehension of most
people who haven't experienced it, and many who have experienced
the absence of the completion, we numb out to avoid the painful
knowledge and feelings associated with the loss that created the
disruption in the first place. As Jane Guttman so aptly put it, "This
deep seated need [often] becomes a blueprint for living."

I have been keenly aware of and have experienced the pain
of the loss of my mother since I was four years old. I was constantly
aware of it either directly or indirectly when it was pre-conscious, sort
of on the "tip of my tongue," but I pushed it away. I had to push it
away in order to survive. It felt like I had to make it not be real. So
I denied it. I didn't tell my friends or wife. It felt like the pain and
sadness would annihilate me, break my heart in two if I let myself

experience the pain. I went to therapy but I refused to discuss adoption. I told my therapist that I was adopted by speaking in metaphors. I told my therapist I would leave on the spot if she mentioned the "A" word. I meant it! I had never said the word adoption or written it in any form ever in my life, and never would, but one day, I found out that it was possible to search for my natural mother. My therapist badgered me for nine months, probably not a coincidental amount of time and finally I went to my first support group meeting. I hid outside, waiting for someone "nice" to go into the building. I followed. I met other adopted people. I found out that I was to be referred to as an adoptee or an adopted person or an adopted adult. Not an adopted child. I actually, for the first time in my life, said the word out loud. I said I was adopted. The world didn't end. That day changed my life forever. I started the process of ceasing to be a victim. I started to talk about my feelings about my losses to my therapist. I sobbed, I yelled, I hurt like I had never consciously hurt before or so I thought. Then the memories of my pain from childhood came back, the constant pain that I had had to put up walls to ward off.

One day in therapy, after a long time in therapy, in the middle of my worst pain ever, my shrink said to me, "Joe, you are finally living." I thought she had lost her mind. I'm writhing in pain, thrashing and flailing so to speak and she tells me I'm living! What nerve! But... I finally understood what she meant. I was feeling my real feelings and surviving. They didn't kill me. I accepted my pain, it was a part of me and showed me the path to continue my feeling and healing. I faced my demons. They felt gargantuan in size, prehistoric and breathing fire. However, my shrink with her infinite patience comforted me with words. That had never happened before, being comforted in my pain. The enormity of my loss was finally acknowledged and I felt more and more pain and I felt better and better in between times.

I have been searching for my birth family for 18 years and have never been able to find any birth relative. I don't know when or where I was born. A Scorpio fits me well, probably born in 1939, probably the late fall or early winter, sold by a baby-seller named Bessie Bernard. I could have been born in New York or Florida or elsewhere. My mother's name might have been Haverman or Habersack, or Wilson and she might have stayed at 677 Lexington Avenue in Manhattan while pregnant with me. She probably knew a doctor named Winklestein, but that's all I have and it's all assumption. I haven't given up, but there isn't much to do with no factual information. I am very angry about my inability to find my natural mother or some other relative. I'm angry at the circumstances that led my mother to believe she couldn't keep me. I channel my anger into my work, helping people, and into many of my physical activities. I have learned how to channel my anger and it truly works. I had thought that if I never found my mother or some other relative, that I would not survive, that I could not be happy. Well, that's what I thought, but the process of searching, being in therapy and going to support group meetings, which I think is the most important of all, has enabled me to heal enough. Enough so that while I still hurt horribly sometimes, I don't experience my hurt as often as I used to. When it does present itself, I embrace it, let it happen to the utmost and it doesn't last as long at all. Most important of all, I'm not afraid of my feelings anymore. They are finally bearable. I am not afraid of my own feelings. If someone told me twenty years ago that I would ever be able to make that last statement, I wouldn't have believed them. But I am not afraid and I know that if YOU do this work you too can stop being afraid of yourself and your feelings. True happiness can only come to those who let themselves feel all of their feelings, the good and the bad. Otherwise, what we think of as happiness may well be the absence of the very uncomfortable feelings. Having a reunion doesn't take away the pain and anger

> My personal story is very unusual so please don't let it discourage you from searching. Most people do succeed in their searches. Most people do not have fictitious birth dates and birth places.

and sadness. Only hard work will do that. Reunions are very very important, of course. However, they are icing on the cake. Even a "bad" reunion has its benefits. At least you "know" your truth, whatever it is. But the process is the most important part... the "Journey of the Adopted Self" is the key to the healing. In eighteen years, I have never met anyone who told me they were sorry they searched. I presume someone must exist who feels that way and that saddens me. Searching *is* truly a win-win situation.

I know that many of you who read this book will be experiencing much pain. Take a moment and count your scars. Be proud of your scars because they are proof of what you have survived.

> "Yes, every place I look, at every face I see, she's on my mind; I've gotta find this part of me. I miss her more, more than before, as time goes by. I'll wonder who my mother is until I die." – *I Wonder Who My Mother Is?* – Gladys Shelley

I hope that you understand that there is hope. The pain and anger and sadness are manageable. You, too, can stop being afraid of your own feelings. You really can! How to do that is my gift to you. I sincerely hope that after reading this book you can unwrap it. It is sent with caring from someone who knows how bad it can be and how good it can be too.

In the words of Louis Mann, "Only eyes washed by tears can see clearly."

About the Author

Joe Soll is a psychotherapist and lecturer internationally recognized as an expert in adoption related issues and a former adjunct professor of social work at Fordham University Graduate School. He is director and co-founder of **Adoption Crossroads** in New York City, a non-profit organization an organization that helps reunite and gives support to adoptees, natural parents and adoptive parents. Adoption Crossroads is affiliated with more than 390 adoption agencies, mental health institutions and adoption search and support groups in eight countries, representing more than 500,000 individuals whose lives have been affected by adoption. **Adoption Crossroads** is also dedicated to educating the public about adoption issues, preserving families and reforming current adoption practices.

The director and founder of the **Adoption Counseling Center** in New York City, Mr. Soll is also co-organizer and co-chair of the **New York State Adoption Agency Task Force**; a member of Matilda Cuomo's 1993 **Advisory Council on the "Adoption Option"**; conference chair and board member of the **American Adoption Congress,** a trustee of the **International Soundex Reunion Registry**, and an advisor to the **Center for Family**

Connections. He's a fellow of the **American Orthopsychiatric Association,** the **American Association of Grief Counselors,** and member of the **Council on Social Work Education**, the **National Association of Social Workers** and the **National Academy of Television Arts and Sciences.**

Since 1989, Mr. Soll has organized and coordinated seven international mental health conferences on adoption for mental health professionals and those affected by adoption. He has been an expert witness in court about adoption related issues and has lectured widely at adoption agencies, social work schools, mental health facilities and mental health conferences in the U.S. and Canada.

Mr. Soll has appeared on radio and television more than 300 times, given more than 130 lectures on adoption related issues and has been featured or quoted in more than three dozen newspapers, books and magazines. In 1994 he was portrayed as a therapist in the NBC made-for-TV movie about adoption, *The Other Mother.* He played himself in the HBO original movie *Reno Finds Her Mom.* He was featured in the 2001 Telly Award winning Global Japan documentary, "Adoption Therapist: Joe Soll."   His own story as an adoptee has been presented more than three dozen times on Unsolved Mysteries. He has walked the 250 miles from New York City to Washington, D.C. six times to create public awareness of the need for adoption reform. He resides in Congers, NY and maintains an office in New York City.